From Zero To Three Hundred

A Bridge Journey

Taken By
James Marsh Sternberg MD (Dr. J)

authorHOUSE

AuthorHouse™
1663 Liberty Drive
Bloomington, IN 47403
www.authorhouse.com
Phone: 833-262-8899

Published by AuthorHouse 02/28/2022

ISBN: 978-1-6655-5351-3 (sc)
ISBN: 978-1-6655-5350-6 (e)

CONTENTS

ACKNOWLEDGMENTS

I would like to thank all my teachers, coaches, partners, and friends who helped make this incredible journey possible.

Special thanks of course to Allan, Stevie, Freddy, and Bernie.

To my editor Paul Linxwiler, who always makes my writing better than it is.

And to Vickie Bader, without whose love and patience I could not have accomplished much of whatever I have done.

James Marsh Sternberg, MD (Dr. J)
Palm Beach Gardens, FL

INTRODUCTION

Three hundred. What's so special about the number 300? It's the magic number all serious bridge players seek, often unsuccessfully. It takes 300 masterpoints of varying types to become a Life Master in the American Contract Bridge League (ACBL).

When I took up the game, I had never played bridge previously but thought it was a game that could be learned in a few weeks and would provide a recreational outlet. I was searching for a new hobby.

Wow, was I in for a surprise! It didn't take long for me to realize it was going to require more than a few weeks to learn. Fortunately, I met one of the foremost bridge teachers in the country, Allan Cokin. Together we began the journey from zero to 300.

This book tells of our adventures as I, studying under and playing with Allan, won 377 masterpoints to become the first player to become Life Master in less than one year, winning the ACBL's Rookie of the Year Award.

This book tells the story of our achievements, the wins, the losses, some exciting hands and hilarious events that can only happen at the bridge table. Travel with me as we play against world famous experts and suffer my blunders with me.

The second half of the book continues with my bridge adventures after achieving Life Master, the ups, the downs, and lots more. I hope you enjoy the book as much as I have enjoyed the journey.

CHAPTER ONE
JANUARY

It was a dark and stormy night. Thunder, lightning, pouring rain, gusting winds. One would have been afraid to venture outside. Actually, it was a beautiful sunny afternoon in South Florida, and I was relaxing by the pool. But all great books seem to start out with a dark and stormy night so there you are.

I had come home from the hospital where I was the chief of the radiology department. It was a few days after New Year's in 1977, and after a full day of looking at x-ray films, not very hard work, I was just taking in some of the Florida sun and drinking a cold beer.

I didn't have much to do. I was living alone in a rental apartment, having been divorced for a few years. I didn't have many hobbies. While I had been a good junior golfer and played on my college golf team at Columbia, my hours at the hospital had pretty much forced my golf game into retirement. But life was good in South Florida.

It was certainly better than in Buffalo, New York, where I had grown up. In Buffalo, they have lots of signs that say, "Go to Florida." When it came down to going to medical school in Syracuse, New York, or Miami, Florida, it was a pretty easy decision. Which would you have chosen?

My father was a physician, He was a general practitioner who spent his entire career in Buffalo. He did not want to move to Florida and be just another old retired guy. He preferred being a well known physician in Buffalo even though it meant making house calls at night on roads covered with ice and snow. I remember our family made occasional visits to Palm Beach, but my father couldn't bring himself to give up his life in Buffalo.

But he had passed away the previous summer, which, of course, only added to my melancholy. I had many good memories of my parents.

One was how every morning, while having breakfast prepared by our live-in housekeeper, my father religiously studied the bridge column in the Courier Express, the Buffalo morning newspaper. My parents both played a lot of bridge together before divorcing while I was in college. There was a social club in downtown Buffalo where my father often went to play bridge with several of my uncles and other friends. I do remember that one of my uncles had a heart attack and had keeled over dead on the table while playing a slam at the club. I had no idea what a slam was. I had occasionally tried to watch, but my parents had no interest in teaching me bridge. I remembered a little bit about taking tricks but that was about it. I thought it was like war, a game I had played as a kid.

While lying around the pool that late afternoon, I thought maybe bridge might be something to occupy some of my free time. The following week I went to a bookstore. You may remember those places where you actually could buy a book rather than download the ePub version as you do today. I bought a copy of Alfred Sheinwold's "Bridge Play" for $2.95 and started scanning thru it. I was completely lost.

I had never played cards as a kid. I had no "card sense." As I later learned, bridge is like golf or tennis. If you start as a kid, you develop a certain sense that's hard to describe, but almost impossible to learn later. A certain feel, in golf it's a certain touch just like in tennis. Good card players who were brought up playing gin rummy and especially pinochle, have a certain indescribable feel for the cards.

It's like trying to learn to play golf or tennis as an adult. Sure, you can learn, but it's the rare exception who reaches the "pro" level. Bridge is very much the same as other sports, as I'll talk about more later. Anyhow, I was ready. After a week or so of reading, I looked up where the bridge clubs were. I was ready to do battle. Or so I thought.

I called the Fort Lauderdale Bridge Club on the east side of the city. I said I wanted to play but didn't have a partner. The director/owner, a very nice lady named Elsie Abrams, told me to come over and she would have a partner for me. They ran 14 games a week. In those days, game times were 1 p.m. and 7 p.m. every day. There were ladies who played 14 times a week.

Their masterpoint totals were more an attendance record than anything else. I met Elsie and she said she had a very nice gentleman for me to play with. "Great, I thought," anxious to try out my newly developed skills. I introduced myself to this not very friendly looking gentleman. He said he had offered to play with me and asked, "What's 1NT–4NT?"

"Blackwood," I announced, proud that I remembered the name of the convention. "Come back after you have learned a little more," he said and walked away.

So much for my first night of playing bridge. I left, totally confused, and not especially happy with this old guy's manners. I later found out he was one of the worst players in the club which of course was why he was available to play. Needless to say, we never did hook up for a game.

So I went home and read some more and a few days later called Elsie again. She apologized for my first experience and said, "I have a really nice guy for you to play with." Encouraged, I cautiously went to the club again. I met a middle-aged man named Bill Doherty from the Boston area who was spending the winter in South Florida. He couldn't have been nicer. I explained I was a complete beginner. Bill said that everybody was a complete beginner at one time or another and he would be more than happy to play with me.

I think we finished a whooping 10th out of 10. If there had been an 11th pair, we would have been 11th. I really felt terrible. But Bill couldn't have been nicer. We went over a few deals and he gave me a few pointers. He even suggested we play again. Maybe he was trying to move up to ninth out of 10, or maybe he was just a masochist. As I recall, we did move up a couple of notches, which only shows how bad the rest of the field was. You would think playing 14 times a week, they might have shown some degree of ability.

Near the end of the month, there was a regional tournament in Sarasota. Regional, sectional, I didn't know the difference between one or the other. But it wasn't a long ride, so off I went by myself. I checked in to the hotel and asked where the bridge tournament was being held. The receptionist gave me directions. I went to the partnership desk and inquired about a partner. "How many masterpoints do you have?" asked a nice lady with a smile. What did I know? No one told me to inflate the number a bit. "None," I replied with a smile on my face, too. Her smile didn't last very long. "Well," she said. "I'm not sure we can find a partner for you." Her prediction came true and after two days of not playing I returned home quite discouraged, about ready to hang it up.

But I was studying hard and amazingly – after a few more games at the Ft. Lauderdale club with Bill, whose patience must have been running thin – we came in first. You would have thought we had won the Bermuda Bowl.

I remember being so excited. We went to Wolfie's restaurant down the street to celebrate our great victory. I was on top of the world. I was a bridge winner, a champion. Wow, amazing. While I was stuffing my mouth with pastrami and everything else on the menu, Bill complimented my improvement and said if I really wanted to improve, I needed to hook up with a good teacher.

A bridge teacher? What's that? I had never heard the term. And he made a suggestion that, looking back, forever changed the course of my life. He said he knew a top-notch teacher from New England who was in town. Would I be interested in taking some lessons? He had nothing to gain in this, but would put me together with this teacher.

What did I know? He could have been fixing me up with the Rueful Rabbit or the Hideous Hog. Fortunately, he introduced me to one of the finest bridge coaches in the country – Allan Cokin. Yes, he would later have some problems with the ACBL in the early 1980's, but after resolution, was well respected and coached many of the great teams until his passing in 2014. I started taking lessons with Allan. Little did I know where this would lead.

CHAPTER TWO
FEBRUARY

So now I had a coach, was taking lessons, and playing a few times a week with Allan. "How would you like to go to the nationals in Pasadena," Allan asked? The Spring North American Bridge Championships in those days were held a bit earlier than they are today. Sure, I thought, why not? At least I'll have a partner. My 12-man group at the hospital could certainly get by without me (well, I was the chief, so...).

Allan and I made plans, but there were no non-stop flights from Fort Lauderdale to Pasadena. We had to change in Dallas and Denver. "What could go wrong," you ask? Well, each stop involved a time change.

We were OK in Dallas, but I can still remember sitting in the Denver airport watching our flight take off as we were munching down on something, having lost track of the time. We finally arrived in Pasadena at 6 a.m. the next morning, with not a lot of sleep.

In those days, the late 70's and early 80's, there was no stratification of bridge events. There was one flight only: Flight A. Trying to win masterpoints in those days meant playing against the big boys or not playing. We played in a Men's two-day pair event.

After the first session, we had something like 410. Games were scored by points, not percentages, and we were leading. Of course, I had no idea what our score meant. This obviously didn't last but I scratched out a few points.

On this deal, I made a play more by luck than skill that made the Daily Bulletin:

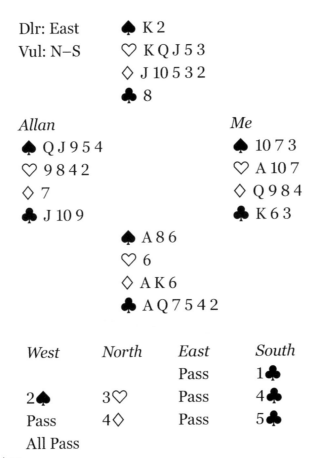

Dlr: East
Vul: N–S

♠ K 2
♡ K Q J 5 3
◇ J 10 5 3 2
♣ 8

Allan
♠ Q J 9 5 4
♡ 9 8 4 2
◇ 7
♣ J 10 9

Me
♠ 10 7 3
♡ A 10 7
◇ Q 9 8 4
♣ K 6 3

♠ A 8 6
♡ 6
◇ A K 6
♣ A Q 7 5 4 2

West	North	East	South
		Pass	1♣
2♠	3♡	Pass	4♣
Pass	4◇	Pass	5♣
All Pass			

Opening Lead: ◇7

Most pairs played in 3NT, some making, some not. This North-South, crowded by Allan's weak jump overcall at favorable vulnerability, landed in the inferior contract of 5♣. The trump position is very favorable and the contract can be made against almost any defense.

Allan found the best opening lead, and declarer played the 10 from dummy. The normal play for East is to duck since it's clear South has the ◇A K, perhaps doubleton. But I covered with the queen. Now the contract was unmakeable. With a diamond ruff being threatened, the best South could do was cross to the ♠K, finesse the ♣Q and clear trumps.

But then the defense could drive out the ♠A, and declarer would lose a spade trick and the ♡A. If East did not cover, South could draw trumps without dislodging the ♠K and make the contract.

We won a few points in Pasadena, but I had a special opportunity. Being with 'Coke,' as Allan was known, I met many of the bridge players my father had only read about. I forged friendships that have lasted even until today. Bob Hamman and Bobby Wolff, Alan Sontag and Peter Weichsel, Bobby Goldman, Bart Bramley, Marty Bergen, Larry Cohen – the list goes on. It was like a golf hacker suddenly having dinner every night telling stories with Palmer or Nicklaus.

After the games, we hung out at the bar or had dinner with the cream of the bridge world, going over the day's hands, telling stories, etc. It was wonderful. I came back to Florida even more determined to try to learn how to play. I was, however, beginning to understand this was not a game one learns in a few months or out of a book. I had to play, make all the mistakes possible, and hopefully learn from them.

Fortunately, my radiology partner was very understanding. I told him I was going to be taking a few more long weekends off than usual this year and why. I was very lucky to have a great partner, Dr. Stephen Schulman, to whom one of my books "When Michaels Met The Unusual" is dedicated. "Sure," he said. "I've got you covered. Take all the time you need."

CHAPTER THREE
MARCH

When I first started, I had no concept of what a masterpoint was. Black, silver, gold: They could have been chartreuse for all I knew. And I had never heard the term Life Master. But I had gotten lucky. By having started playing in January as a complete novice, I was an official "Rookie." Because I had joined the ACBL in January, I was automatically eligible for the Rookie of the Year contest and had a full 12 months to compete. But this was the last thing on my mind. I played in lots of club games, mostly at the Fort Lauderdale Bridge Club and in a few sectional tournaments, but masterpoints were not on my mind.

At the annual Miami Regional in the spring, Coke and I had a section first in a Men's Pairs and a third-place finish in a Men's Swiss Teams. In those days, Men's and Women's events were still being held as separate events. It was still a few years away from the lawsuit that forced the elimination of Men's events, leaving only Open and Women's events and some Mixed events.

At that tournament, I vividly remember spending each morning at the pool, listening to the great Al Roth telling stories. I was fortunate to be included in the gang. Those were lessons you could not find in any book. Al Roth was the greatest. He invented everything in bridge; negative doubles, weak two-bids – the list goes on.

One night, we were going to dinner with Al. There were about five or six of us in the car. Someone would give Al a hand and ask him what he would bid. Al would answer and a voice from the back seat, Vic Zeve, would promptly say, "That's my bid!" About five or six hands went by with Al answering, followed by "That's my bid!" from the back seat.

Finally with the next question, Al turned to Vic in the back and asked "Hey Vic, what would you bid?" Vic gave some answer and Al said "That's the worst bid I ever heard." They asked Al what he would bid and he answered. From the back came, "That was my second choice!"

CHAPTER FOUR
APRIL

I continued to study and play locally but hadn't won anything. Masterpoints and becoming a Life Master were not even a thought. I was just trying not to be the worst player in the room.

In a local sectional Swiss team event, I was playing with the late Jim Beery, a fine player who was the engineer for the WOR radio station. After the last session each day, we used to go to dinner with our teammates at this local restaurant with an all-you-can-eat buffet. Beery was a big guy and could pack it in. Finally, the manager, after watching Beery in action at the buffet, came over and said, "If you all will leave now, there will be no charge. Your friend is putting us out of business."

Sometimes, a little knowledge can be a dangerous thing. Look at this deal. I was South, Beery was North.

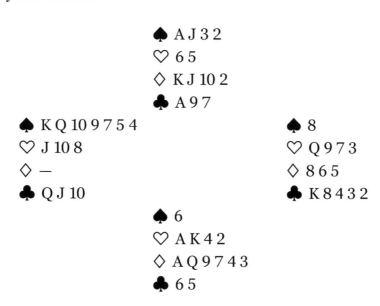

♠ A J 3 2
♡ 6 5
◇ K J 10 2
♣ A 9 7

♠ K Q 10 9 7 5 4
♡ J 10 8
◇ —
♣ Q J 10

♠ 8
♡ Q 9 7 3
◇ 8 6 5
♣ K 8 4 3 2

♠ 6
♡ A K 4 2
◇ A Q 9 7 4 3
♣ 6 5

West	North	East	South
			1♦
4♠	4NT	Pass	6♦
All Pass			

West led the ♠K. At all the other tables, North doubled 3♠ or 4♠ and took five or six tricks on defense. But Beery not unreasonably tried for slam. You can see I have 10 top tricks plus two heart ruffs in dummy for 12. How did I explain to my teammates how I managed to go down one?

Well, easy. We were playing against two very nice little old ladies. I reasoned if she did have her eight-card spade suit, the only way to go down was to play the ♠A at trick one and have East ruff. By ducking, I could win trick two and later discard my club loser on the ♠A.

You couldn't trust anyone those days. I ducked – down one. Just great!

Another player who had a big influence on my career was the late Bernie Chazen. He was an expert player, teacher and writer. Many years later, he published a bi-monthly magazine called Bridge Sense. Years later, I became his editor. He and Coke were almost always on the same wavelength when it came to bidding theory and systems.

This made it very easy for me. While I had little card sense, I was good at learning bridge systems. I could remember conventions and studied the many pages of notes they gave me. I rarely got anything wrong from a point of remembering. Correct hand evaluation of course was another thing because I was a neophyte.

One treatment we played involved our three-level responses to our 1NT openings.

> 1NT–3♣ = 5–5 minors, game-only interest
> 　3♦ = Where is your shortness?
> 　　3♡ = Lower, hearts
> 　　3♠ = Higher, spades

> 1NT– 3♦ = 5–5 minors, slammish
> 　3♡ = Where is your shortness?
> 　　3♠ = Lower, hearts
> 　　3NT = Higher, spades, non-forcing
> 　　4♣ = Higher, spades, forcing

Chazen and I were playing in a sectional Swiss when this deal arose:

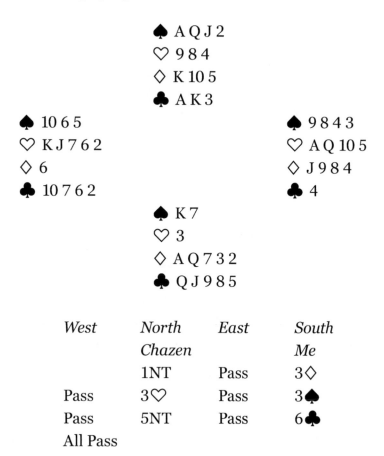

♠ A Q J 2
♡ 9 8 4
◇ K 10 5
♣ A K 3

♠ 10 6 5
♡ K J 7 6 2
◇ 6
♣ 10 7 6 2

♠ 9 8 4 3
♡ A Q 10 5
◇ J 9 8 4
♣ 4

♠ K 7
♡ 3
◇ A Q 7 3 2
♣ Q J 9 8 5

West	North	East	South
	Chazen		Me
	1NT	Pass	3◇
Pass	3♡	Pass	3♠
Pass	5NT	Pass	6♣
All Pass			

I chose 6♣ because of the stronger intermediates in clubs. Notice 6◇ would have failed with the 4–1 trump break. There was nothing to the play. After ruffing the second heart, I drew trumps and claimed. We scored heavily on this deal, a good one for our system.

CHAPTER FIVE
MAY

I continued to take lessons and play club games with Coke, and we decided to try another regional. We went to Roanoke, Virginia. In those days, the schedule every week was mostly a pair game starting on a Tuesday or Wednesday, continuing thru Saturday, and then a Swiss team event on Sunday. Knockout events were rare. Every event was Flight A – good luck! At every table you were facing some hot shot player or pair. Trying to win anything against those players was tough. But we had a section first in one of the Men's Pairs, and then came the Swiss team event on Sunday.

Our team consisted of Coke and myself, Tony "The Kas" Kasday, Marc "Jake" Jacobus and Stevie "Wonder" Sion. A real cast of characters. But the bridge gods were shining on us that day, and I won my first regional title. It was certainly cause for a big celebratory dinner. I was floating on air. A regional? Really?

I thought back to the day when I won my first club game with Bill Doherty and went to Wolfies to celebrate, thinking that would be the biggest win of my life. Little did I know the floodgates were about to open.

By now, I had accumulated about 80 masterpoints. And for the first time, I began to realize that by having started from scratch in January, I was eligible for an award I had never heard of called "Rookie of the Year." Looking up the statistics from a few previous years showed the winners averaged about 150–180 points. Maybe I could come close?

CHAPTER SIX
JUNE AND JULY

During the summer of 1977, I was busy at the hospital and played a bit less. In June, I went to Tulsa, Oklahoma, and picked up a few points: a section first in an Open Pairs. While playing in this event and sitting North–South, with two boards each round, we did have a fun incident.

An elderly couple, probably married, came to our table. Cokin opened 1NT on the first board and the woman overcalled 2♡. She ended playing in 2♡ doubled and went minus 500. The husband started screaming, "How could you bid 2♡ with that hand?" He wouldn't stop, just going at her with both barrels. Cokin kept saying, "Sir, we have another board to play." We finally calmed him down. But Cokin, instead of bringing up the second board, just turned the first board around. Now I opened 1NT and yes, the husband bid 2♡. But knowing where the cards were, we got him for minus 800. Justice!

In Winnipeg, Canada, I finished third in a knockout event. We lost one of our teammates at the U.S.–Canada border. He had no identification other than a pencil from the Boston Chess Club. "You can call them," he told the border authorities. "Everybody there knows me."

What brought me to attention, however, was an article in the ACBL's Bridge Bulletin later in the summer headlined: "Dr. Sternberg Leads For Rookie of Year." Who, me? It said I had a healthy 36-point lead at the halfway mark in the race for Rookie of the Year honors in the ACBL. I had accumulated 110 masterpoints, and my nearest challenger had 74.

Well, this certainly perked up my interest. Work at the hospital would have to wait. I had plenty of radiology partners who could cover.

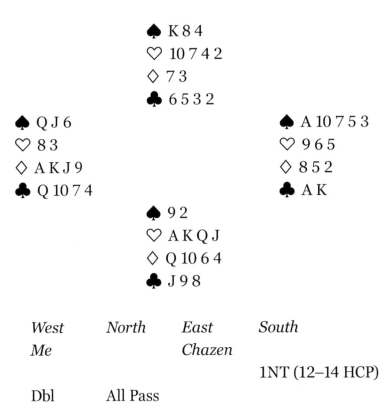

Dr. Sternberg Leads For Rookie of Year

Dr. J. H. Sternberg of Plantation FL has a healthy 36-point lead at the halfway mark in the race for Rookie of the Year honors in the ACBL. Dr. Sternberg, who had fewer than 5 master points at the start of 1977, had earned 110 by the end of June.

Listed below are the 15 leading point winners in each category from rookie through Life Master:

Rookie [0-5 Points] of the Year

1. Dr. J.H. Sternberg, Plantation FL	110
2. M. Moss, Williamsburg VA	74
3. R.D. Thomson, Berkeley CA	69
4. Miss M.E. Zaklama, Webster NY	60
5. Mrs. L. Levey, Toronto	54
6. G. Mantell, Morgantown WV	53
7. P. Santino, Brooklyn	53
8. P.S. Kushner, Berkeley CA	50
9. B.C. Kishpaugh, Arvada CO	49
10. Mrs. H.C. Buettner, Farmington Hills MI	48
11. Mrs. D. Kohen, Toronto	47
12. R.B. Voss, Macomb IL	46
13. J.E. Thirkill, San Diego	46
14. Mrs. A. Korf, Englewood CO	45
15. A. Colas, New York City	44

I played in a sectional Swiss team where we finished poorly, but this interesting deal came up:

```
                    ♠ K 8 4
                    ♡ 10 7 4 2
                    ◇ 7 3
                    ♣ 6 5 3 2
♠ Q J 6                              ♠ A 10 7 5 3
♡ 8 3                                ♡ 9 6 5
◇ A K J 9                            ◇ 8 5 2
♣ Q 10 7 4                           ♣ A K
                    ♠ 9 2
                    ♡ A K Q J
                    ◇ Q 10 6 4
                    ♣ J 9 8
```

West	North	East	South
Me		Chazen	
			1NT (12–14 HCP)
Dbl	All Pass		

14

I led the ◇A and Bernie played the deuce. I switched to a low club. Bernie won and returned a diamond. Back came another club and another diamond. I cashed two more clubs and a good diamond. On those three winners, Bernie discarded three low hearts. Next came the ♠Q and you can see what happened. We took all 13 tricks.

Bernie in his usual exuberant style, raised a fist, giving a loud, "Yes sir!" This was heard at the other table where our teammates had already played the board. "What was that," asked an opponent? Coke said "It sounds like 1NT doubled down seven!"

Years later, when Jim Jacoby wrote up this hand for the Fort Lauderdale Sun-Sentinel, he wrote "Occasionally the weak 1NT bidder must pay a price ... I have never been doubled at 1NT and failed to take a trick."

CHAPTER SEVEN
AUGUST THRU OCTOBER

It was time to turn the heat up. We had two big weeks. In August, in Overland Park, Kansas, we had a section first in both a Master's Pairs and a Men's Pairs, a sixth place in an Open Pairs, and finished second in both the knockout and the Men's Swiss. My fondest memory of that week however, was playing tennis every morning with the late Bobby Goldman, the Hall of Famer who died in 1999. He was one of the nicest guys on tour, and, of course, a legend as a bridge player. I was a novice, yet he went out of his way to be so nice. His passing at a young age was a tragedy.

In October, we went to Albany, New York, and had another good week. In the Men's Pairs we finished seventh. Today, you wouldn't think twice about having finished seventh, but in those days with only Flight A, it was significant and paid "something." We were fifth in the knockout, eighth in the Master Swiss, and then hit a home run by winning the Open Swiss.

The points were starting to add up. I didn't know where I stood in the race for Rookie, but felt I had to be at or very near the top. As we were approaching November, the thought of becoming a Life Master began to creep into the conversations.

What does Life Master mean? While it is the dream of every new aspiring serious bridge player, some never make it in their lifetime. To become a Life Master (LM), a player must win a specified number of masterpoints at different levels of play, including major bridge tournaments. The rank of Life Master was created in 1936. The first Life Master was David Bruce. Then came Oswald Jacoby and Harold Schenken. Initially it took only 10 Master Points to become a Life Master. Of course, points were much harder to win. For example, 2 points were awarded for winning the prestigious Vanderbilt, and 1 point for finishing second. By 1978, players won 240 and 105 points for first and second.

Between 1940 and 1944, the ACBL deducted up to 10 point a year from players who did not participate and win tournaments. Hence by this method, Master Points provided a better guide to a player's current ability. This practice of deducting points is no longer in effect.

As a measure of how inflated points have become, let's compare these two charts. In 1975, a list of the top ten Life Masters lifetime point totals showed Barry Crane as the leader with 19,611 and Paul Soloway in tenth position with 10,918. No player could have attained this many points without extraordinary ability.

By way of contrast, and as a measure of how inflation has affected Master Points, in 2002 the leader Paul Soloway had 56,513 and Fred Hamilton in tenth place had 28,770. Can you imagine what the players from the 40's and 50's would think if they could see these numbers?

Today one needs a total of 300 masterpoints (or 500 if a player joined the ACBL after January 2010), of which a certain percentage must be won at major events like regional tournaments, not just club games. A masterpoint was supposed to be a measure of achievement in bridge competition.

What was the big deal about being a Life Master all about? In the early days, perhaps until the mid-1980's or so, masterpoints were more difficult to come by. Then came a system called stratification. Players were divided into Flights A, B or C depending on how many points they had. And then there were separate events. You could play in Flight B or Flight C, where there was an upper limit on the number of points a player could have. Also, knockout events became the rage, a new one starting almost every day of the tournament week. And these, too, were flighted.

What was the result of this? One was that the number of masterpoints being awarded suddenly jumped like a rocket being launched. The second effect was that now one could become a Life Master without ever having had to play against a Life Master. Events like the Gold Rush contests, limited to players with 750 points, awarded the precious Gold points needed to become a Life Master.

Also the knockout events had many flights, sometimes six, seven or more, all of which paid gold points. There were many players with more than 300 or 500 masterpoints, but lacked the required 'color' points. Now, one could win the necessary Gold by playing in lower flights. Points flowed like water from a tap.

CHAPTER EIGHT
NOVEMBER

Atlanta was the site of the Fall North American Bridge Championships.

I didn't know it at the time, but I was up to 260 masterpoints and had won the necessary number of gold points.

Steve Sion and I entered the two-session Open Pairs. There were 785 pairs, 26 sections in all. These were the days of Flight A only, take it or leave it. In the afternoon session, we won our section scoring 196½, average being 156. Those days scores were not by percentages but by points. Here was a deal that helped us:

```
                    ♠ J 10 9 4
                    ♡ 10 6 5
                    ◇ 7 4 3
                    ♣ 5 4 3
     ♠ 3                              ♠ K 7 6 2
     ♡ K J 9 7 3                      ♡ —
     ◇ K Q 8 5                        ◇ J 10 6 2
     ♣ K Q 2                          ♣ A 10 9 8 7
                    ♠ A Q 8 5
                    ♡ A Q 8 4 2
                    ◇ A 9
                    ♣ J 6
```

West	North	East	South
Me		Sion	
		Pass	1♡
Pass	Pass	Dbl	1♠
Dbl	All Pass		

18

East reopened on his distribution, and South bid 1♠. I doubled showing I had a heart stack and would have bid earlier if not for the 1♡ bid. Steve decided to let South sweat it out.

I led the ♣K Q and switched to the ◇K to declarer's ace. He exited a diamond to my queen and I returned a diamond, declarer ruffing. Declarer was stuck in his hand and led the ♠Q, ducked. He tried the ♡A. East ruffed and returned a trump. When the smoke cleared, declarer had only three trump tricks, a ruff and the ◇A for minus 500.

In the evening session, we turned it up a notch, bidding 6NT, 7NT, and 7♣, worth 11, 11 ½, and 12 points respectively, finishing with a rip-roaring 220½ for 417 total, coming in first overall by four matchpoints ahead of second. In those days, everything was scored by hand. With 26 sections to score, we had a long wait before they posted the results. WOW!

Winning was worth 50 masterpoints, pushing me to 310. That was amazing. Winning team games is one thing, but to win a Flight A pair game at the nationals, with 26 sections, shows how good my partner was. It certainly wasn't me, although I guess I made fewer mistakes than usual plus we must have had help from the opponents.

In the Daily Bulletin, Editor Henry Francis wrote a glowing article and coined the nickname "Dr. J" which has stuck with me ever since, even being listed as such in the Encyclopedia of Bridge.

We must have been on a good roll. The next day, we played in another two-session smaller pair game and finished second, capping off an amazing week.

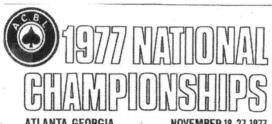

1977 NATIONAL CHAMPIONSHIPS

NOVEMBER 18-27 ATLANTA

ATLANTA, GEORGIA   NOVEMBER 18-27, 1977

VOL. 51, No. 4   Monday, November 21, 1977

ON JANUARY 1, 1977, Dr. Jim Sternberg of Fort Lauderdale had zero master points --
he wasn't even a member of the ACBL. In fact, he hardly even knew how to play bridge.
Today Dr. J is a Life Master. To the best of our knowledge, the Florida radiologist is
the only player in history without a bridge background to start from scratch and make it
all the way to Life Master in less than a year. And he did it with flair! He and Steve Sion
of Waban MA had a rip-roaring 220 1/2 last night to win the 758-pair Open Pair championship. That was worth 50 points -- and he needed only 40. In fact, 260 of Jim's 310 points
are either red or gold, and he actually won three regional events this year.

It all started when he met Bill Doherty from Cape Cod at a Fort Lauderdale club --
"I dropped in because I was looking for something to do," said Dr. J, "and Bill told me
about tournaments. I went to one in St. Petersburg and presented myself at the partnership desk. They asked me how many points I had, and I told them zero. You can imagine
the partners I got! But I heard about Allan Cokin, and got together with him. He introduce
me to Steve Sion and I've been playing the circuit with them this year. They're a pair of
super teachers -- don't ever let anybody tell you any different."

Steve and Allan (who incidentally finished in second place in the Open yesterday)
tell it differently. "Dr. J plays a good game," said Steve. "He bids well and he is imaginative. The teacher can't win unless the pupil is a good learner." As examples, Steve
cited three hands from last night's session -- they got to 6NT, 7NT and 7C, worth 11,
11 1/2 and 12 points respectively.

The American Contract Bridge League

presents this

Life Master Certificate

to

James Marsh Sternberg

in recognition
of outstanding achievement
in bridge competition

1977

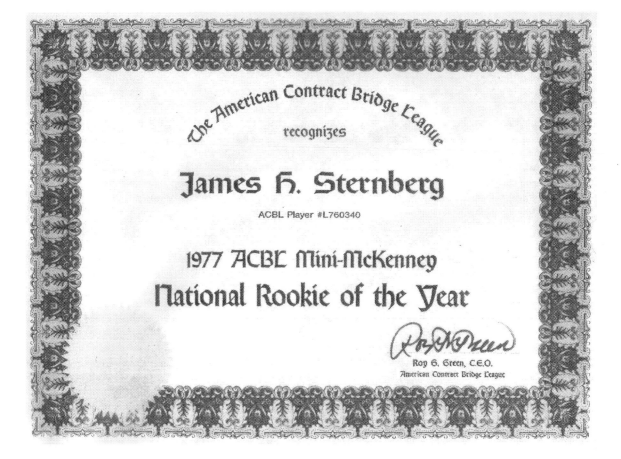

The American Contract Bridge League

recognizes

James H. Sternberg

ACBL Player #L760340

1977 ACBL Mini-McKenney
National Rookie of the Year

Roy G. Green, C.E.O.
American Contract Bridge League

Fort Lauderdale News and Sun-Sentinel, Sunday, Dec. 4, 1977

Bridge
By Charles Whitebrook

LIFE MASTER IN 11 MONTHS

Last Jan. 1, Dr. Jim Sternberg of Fort Lauderdale had zero master points. He wasn't even a member of the ACBL. In fact, he hardly even knew how to play bridge. Today Dr. J. is a Life Master.

The Florida radiologist is the only player in history without a bridge background to start from scratch and make it all the way to Life Master in less than a year.

He went to the ACBL Fall Nationals in Atlanta last week needing only 40 Master Points to achieve his L.M. status. So, with partner Steve Sion of Waban, Mass., he proceeded to beat 758 pairs and win the Regional open pair Championships, worth 50 points! Then, to prove he wasn't fooling, he went on a couple of days later to finish second in the National Open Pairs, flight B.

Dr. Jim has also won three other regional titles this year with local expert Allan Cokin, who finished second behind Jim in the first event, and who introduced him to Sion. He claims they're a pair of super teachers. Says Steve: "Dr. J. plays a good game. He bids well and is imaginative. No teacher can win unless the pupil is a good learner."

So, congratulations to Broward's newest Life Master!

Florida
BRIDGE NEWS
FEBRUARY, 1978
Vol. 24. No. 2

STERNBERG IS NATIONAL ROOKIE OF THE YEAR

On January 1, 1977, Dr. Jim Sternberg of Ft. Lauderdale had 0 master points, had virtually no working knowledge of the game of bridge, and had only recently joined the A.C.B.L. In the next 11 months, Dr. J. (as he is affectionately known in the bridge world) won over 350 master points, more than 300 of which were red or gold. Included were 3 regional wins, one of which was a first place in the 758 pair Open at the Atlanta Nationals which put him over the top. To prove this was no fluke, two days later Jim finished 2nd overall in the Flighted Open. He also has 3 regional seconds to his credit.

To put Jim's accomplishments in perspective, it should be pointed out that well over 95% of the A.C.B.L. members have not scored 3 regional wins in their whole careers.

Dr. J's approach to the game is essentially Roth-Stonish—5-card majors, forcing no trump, very sound openings in 1st and 2nd seat. Among his favorite conventions are Flannery, Landy and Michaels.

Jim's advice to people starting out in bridge: "Listen to the advice of your teachers; don't get discouraged; and devote as much time to the game as you possibly can."

Florida
BRIDGE NEWS
MAY, 1978
Vol. 24, No. 3

ACBL ANNUAL AWARDS
(Florida Unit)
Category A—Rookie of the Year—1977

L76-034-0	Dr. J.H. Sternberg	377.16
374-525-2	Mr. J.P. Kichline	88.36
359-391-6	Mr. K.M. Laham	61.66

The Paul Remlinger Memorial Trophy

Kirk Benson won the Paul Remlinger Memorial Trophy for the most master points won in ACBL sanctioned events for 1977 by a Unit 128 member. His total was 442 master points. Carol Ohmann was second with 417 and the National Rookie of the year, Dr. Jim Sternberg, was third with 377.

FEBRUARY 1978

ROOKIE OF THE YEAR [0-5 MPs]

Dr. Jim Sternberg, Ft. Lauderdale FL	377
J. Mureness, Berkeley CA	185
R.D. Thomson, Berkeley CA	156
S. Purdom, Decatur GA	127
Miss M.E. Zakiama, Webster NY	125
Ken Dang, Prince George BC	111

LITTLE McKENNEY RACES
Dr. Sternberg Rookie of Year

Dr. Jim Sternberg of Fort Lauderdale FL wasn't even a League member at the start of 1977, but less than 11 months later he became a Life Master at the Fall North American Championships at Atlanta. By winning 377 points for the year, Dr. J easily won Rookie of the Year honors — he had more than double the total of the runner-up.

To the best of our knowledge, Dr. J is the only player in history without a bridge background to start from scratch and achieve Life Masterhood in less than a year. For more biographical information on the radiologist, see the Atlanta report (p. 20, January 1978 BULLETIN).

Dr. James Sternberg

... an LM at the start of 1977

1977 MAJOR OVERALL TOURNAMENT RECORD

Pasadena Spring Nationals-

	Open Swiss	Fourteenth
Miami-	Mens Swiss	Third
	Mens Pairs	Section First
Roanoke-	*MENS SWISS*	FIRST
	Mens Pairs	Section First
Kansas City-	Knockout Teams	Second
	Mens Swiss	Second
	Open Pairs	Sixth
	Mens Pairs	Section First
	Masters Pairs	Section First
Tulsa-	Knockout Teams	Ninth
	Open Pairs	Section First
Albany-	Knockout Teams	Fifth
	Mens Pairs	Seventh
	OPEN SWISS	FIRST
	Master Swiss	Eighth
Winnepeg-	Knockout Teams	Third

Atlanta Fall Nationals-

	OPEN PAIRS	FIRST
	Open Pairs (A-D)	Second
Nashville-	Open Swiss	Second

CHAPTER NINE
DECEMBER

December was anti-climactic after all that happened in November. We went to Nashville, Tennessee, and finished second in the Open Swiss. I finished the year with 377 masterpoints and won the ACBL's National Rookie of the Year award. The next closest total was 185 by J. Mureness of Berkeley, California. The previous high total for the Rookie category was Carolyn Bahr who had won 176 points in 1976.

What made it special was that I was the only player in bridge history without a bridge background to start from scratch and become a Life Master in less than one year. The 377 points stood as a record for over 20 years. No one came close. Alan Kleist won 262 in 1980 and Joe Barnard won 295 points in 1983. In fact, John Blubaugh won in 1987 with only 141 points. Then the floodgates opened and masterpoints started pouring out, hence the need to raise the magic Life Master number from 300 to 500. My record was surpassed around 1998.

Had other players achieved Life Master in a short time? Yes, but with significant bridge backgrounds. The first was Jeremy Flint of England in 1966. He had played mainly in Europe, was a recognized world-class player having won more events than there is space to list here. He joined the ACBL in 1966 and became a Life Master in 10 weeks, playing mostly with the American expert Peter Pender.

Flint passed away in 1989, just a few weeks before the German star player Sabine Zenkel (now Auken) joined the ACBL in October. Playing mostly with the American expert, the late Ron Andersen, she achieved the rank of Life Master after eight weeks of play – 53 days.

In 1996, the Icelandic expert Jakon Kristinsson came to the United States to visit his friend Hjordis Eythorsdottir. He joined the ACBL on June 4, 1996, and in a whirlwind of bridge, playing with Eythorsdottir, Curtis Cheek, Brian Gunnell, and Julie Bradley, became a Life Master in 43 days on July 17, 1996.

So after an exciting journey, zero to over 300, now what?

CHAPTER TEN
LIFE AFTER LM

1977 had certainly had been an exciting year. What started out as looking for a pastime to spend some spare time had turned into a whirlwind adventure. I had traveled the country, made a lot of new friends, was a mini-celebrity (I even had a few bridge groupies hanging around at the tournaments), and was on a first-name basis with all the players my father had only read about with his morning coffee.

My regret, of course, was that my father was not around to enjoy my new adventure with me. I would have really enjoyed introducing him to all the top players. I'm sure he would have been very proud of my success.

But the year had only whetted my appetite. I wanted to learn to play and realized that what I originally thought would take a few weeks would take a few years. I no longer cared if I won another masterpoint. What was I going to do with them? Sell them or leave them to my kids? But the only way to improve was to continue to take lessons and play with better players. And having played with some of the best, I wanted to continue to do the same.

Sure, one hears or reads about clients or sponsors, whatever they were called, "buying" masterpoints by hiring pros. I'm sure that there were many who did and still do today. I wanted to improve, to help my team or partner win, but couldn't care less if I ever won another masterpoint. I wanted to become a player and fortunately I had the time and means to do so.

Let me share with you some stories from 1977 to the present time.

CHAPTER ELEVEN
FRIENDS

Left to Right
Michael Seamon, Dr J
Alan Sontag, Allan Cokin

Pictured above is Michael Seamon, with Alan Sontag & Cokin. He was one of the nicest guys in the game, one of the truly great players. His passing in 2017 at such a young age was such a loss.

Geir Helgemo
and Jim

The Great One
Mr. Alvin Roth

Helge, one of the nicest guys   The great Al Roth & Bernie Chazen

Mike Cappelletti, Sr

Capp always had a cigar, he should have named his convention "Cigar."

Pictured below is "Claude," made famous through the Bridge Bulletin column by George Jacobs. Yes, there really is a Claude! He is not a figment of George's imagination. I enjoyed many games with him during my summers in Chicago.

Jim and John Solodar

"DISA"

Jim and Arnie Fisher

The Famous 'Claude' Vogel

Left to Right
Alan Sontag,
P.O. Sundelin, Jim

John "The Hopper" Solodar, Arnie Fisher, & Disa P O Sundelin

Left to Right
Allan Cokin, Jim Beery
Jack Schwenke, Dr J

Jim Beery and Jack Schwenke

Fred Hamilton and The Doctah

Freddy Hamilton

CHAPTER TWELVE
THE LATER YEARS

Over the next few years, I continued to take lessons, study, and play in tournaments as often as possible. In 1978, I put more time in at the hospital but did win two regionals. But 1979 was a big year. Besides winning six regionals,

I won my first NABC national championship, the Men's Board-A-Match Teams.

Our team from the 1979 Men's Board-A-Match National Championship, my first national championship title: Peter Weichsel, Alan Sontag, Allan Cokin, and myself.

Later I won the District 9 (Florida) Grand National Teams which was played in Orlando, our team consisted of Bruce Ohmann, Larry Griffey, Sion, Coke and myself. We added Bobby Levin for the Zonals, but failed to advance. I have vague memories of playing poorly in Orlando in the first half. While sitting out the second half, I went to Disney and rode on some monster terrifying roller coaster. I rode it over and over, again and again, almost like a death wish. I was so upset with my play, but my teammates pulled out a close win.

30

During those years, I was fortunate to play on teams with Mark Molson, an expert player from Montreal. He was one of the nicest guys in the bridge world and his death from a bleeding aneurysm at a young age was a tragedy.

Also, expert Fred Hamilton had moved to South Florida, and I started a partnership with him that has lasted till the present time. His influence on my bridge career cannot be measured. I owe him so much.

I played a lot with the Bernie Chazen, now deceased, a great player and one of the most popular bridge teachers in South Florida. He was a great character, loud, very funny, loved by everyone. We had so many adventures together. We always went to the Fall NABC tournament on Thanksgiving day and, of course, all restaurants were closed except for the Chinese ones. Bernie and I were always the only Caucasians; we would usually sit with the other patrons and eat whatever they were ordering. We had a lot of success and some near misses.

At one NABC, the Daily Bulletin wrote up this hand under the title "On The Ropes." The editor wrote "When your back is to the wall, sometimes you've just got to pray for a miracle, divine intervention — something."

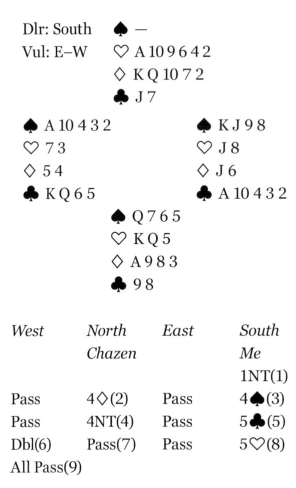

Dlr: South
Vul: E–W

North
♠ —
♡ A 10 9 6 4 2
♢ K Q 10 7 2
♣ J 7

West
♠ A 10 4 3 2
♡ 7 3
♢ 5 4
♣ K Q 6 5

East
♠ K J 9 8
♡ J 8
♢ J 6
♣ A 10 4 3 2

South
♠ Q 7 6 5
♡ K Q 5
♢ A 9 8 3
♣ 9 8

West	North	East	South
	Chazen		Me
			1NT(1)
Pass	4◇(2)	Pass	4♠(3)
Pass	4NT(4)	Pass	5♣(5)
Dbl(6)	Pass(7)	Pass	5♡(8)
All Pass(9)			

The editor continued: "As it is difficult to express perspiration in a bidding diagram, suffice it to say that all of Chazen's bids after 4◇ were made with his fingers crossed ... the faint of heart might consider whether they should read the footnotes."

(1) 10–12 HCP (an experiment at favorable)
(2) Intended as a Texas Transfer to 4♡
(3) Taken as South African Texas, showing spades
(4) Roman Keycard Blackwood for spades. A suit bid would have been Exclusion Blackwood, asking for outside keycards
(5) One or four keycards
(6) Reminding himself to lead a club
(7) An unspoken "thank you," asking for other values
(8) Cuebid, showing heart values
(9) Whew, as you can see, 5♡ made on the nose

OK, you would think we had learned our lesson and stopped all this fancy footwork. Nope, not Bernie. It didn't take long for this "On The Ropes Again" to come up in a local sectional:

North	South
♠ A 10 8 7	♠ Q 6
♡ K 9	♡ A Q J 10 4 3 2
◇ Q 10 9	◇ K J
♣ Q 6 4 2	♣ K J

Bernie	Dr. J
1NT (1)	4♡ (2)
4♠ (3)	5♣ (4)
5♡ (5)	Pass (6)

(1) 10–12 HCP (Haven't learned our lesson yet)
(2) To play; 4♣ would have been a transfer to 4♡
(3) Taken as Texas, showing spades
(4) Exclusion Roman Keycard (excluding clubs), hoping for no keycards, playing 1 or 4, 3 or 0
(5) Cue bid, thinking 5♣ was a cue bid
(6) Thank you. Again, 5♡ made on the nose.

I think it was at this point we stopped playing 10–12 notrumps.

Ever since Henry Francis gave me the nickname Dr. J, it stuck. I'm told only one other person has their nickname in the book, but I don't know who. Nicknames are common in bridge. Many of the top players had them.

One sectional Swiss teams I was playing with Chazen and Cokin was with a client named Evelyn. She was legendary; you could not make up the stories about the things she did at the table. Once, after messing up a deal, the opponents erred by offering her a ruff/sluff. We have all seen or done this ourselves, ruffing in the wrong hand and sluffing from the other. Evelyn took no chances; she ruffed in both hands, creating a play known as a ruff/ruff, never seen before. The look on the defenders' faces must have been priceless.

Anyhow, in this event, Evelyn was on lead after a 1NT–3NT auction and led the ♠ 7. The declarer won the jack and ran off nine tricks.
Evelyn said. "I think we could have done better."
Cokin, having not seen the whole deal yet which had gone very quickly, said "I think he always had nine tricks."
"Well," said Evelyn, "My spades were pretty good."
Cokin asked, "What exactly did you have?"
She replied, "♠AKQ7532."
"You led the ♠ 7?" asked Cokin incredulously.
"Sure, fourth best," was the reply.
Cokin of course was speechless, the declarer having won the first trick with his ♠J 4.
"Could you maybe have tried the ace first," he asked?
"That's the trouble with you experts," complained Evelyn. "You teach me to lead fourth best, then yell at me when I do."

Chazen gave a lecture called, "The Penalty Double is Dead" discussing low-level doubles. Some time later, I was playing with a lady who had attended Bernie's lecture. On one deal after a long tortuous auction with silent opponents, they reached 5♣. I doubled and she bid 5◊. Yes, when I asked her later, you got it – Bernie said, "The penalty double was dead, so ..."

It's tough being a bridge teacher. I'm glad I'm a radiologist.

In the early 80's, we always went in the spring to Miami Beach to play in the Southeasterns, which in those days was a big regional. It was held in the old Americana hotel in Bal Harbor. Al Roth held court on the beach every morning. In charge of the regional was a man named Jeff Glick. He ruled with an iron hand; no fooling around, no nonsense at "his" event.

Of course, we decided to test him out. I had T-shirts made for my Swiss team. On the front it read "Dr. J and the Jews" and on the back were the players' nicknames, like a basketball or football jersey. I, of course, was "The Doctah", Cokin was "Coke', Jacobus was "Jake," Sion was "Wonder," and his girlfriend was "Wonder Woman."

We all got up on a table and sang "The Dr. J Fight Song," 3NT, to the tune of "Ain't She Sweet." Some of the verses:

> No suits stopped, we got no suits stopped.
> Still we bid a very confident 3NT.
>
> We never bid a slam, we just don't give a damn.
> Cause we play every Goddamn hand in 3NT.
>
> We don't make penalty doubles,
> They're just too darn much trouble.
> We play every Goddamn hand in 3NT.
>
> So come and kibbitz our team.
> It really is a scream.
> We play every Goddamn hand in 3NT.

Jeff Glick went ballistic, of course, and wanted to ban us from the event. I still have my T-shirt. Who knows? I might need it again.

Sion and Cokin got in lots of trouble with the ACBL. They were first barred, then reinstated, then Sion was out of bridge, but before that, was the 1984 Spingold.

In the next chapter is the whole amazing story. Read on.

CHAPTER THIRTEEN
THE 1984 SPINGOLD

Washington DC, 1984, a tournament that will "live in infamy," was like no other. Every time I see Larry Cohen he reminds me about it. But more on that later.

The Spingold is a six-day event and one of the three most prestigious events in bridge in the United States. The Vanderbilt and Reisinger are the other two. On the first day, allegations of improprieties led to the withdrawal of an entire team. As Alan Truscott later wrote in the New York Times on July 25, 1985, this was "quickly overshadowed by an event that put bridge, for the first time since a cheating scandal at the world championships in 1965, on the front page of most newspapers."

Edith Rosenkrantz, wife of Dr. George Rosenkrantz of Mexico City, the head of Syntex and the inventor of the birth control pill, had been kidnapped. George was a leading player and captain of one of the highest-seeded teams in the event.

The Washington police and FBI were everywhere. You couldn't tell the cops from the players. George was playing with Eddie Wold as his partner and the rest of his six-man team wasn't too shabby. The rest of his team consisted of Jeff Meckstroth, Eric Rodwell, Marty Bergen and Larry Cohen. This was not exactly a foresome you would like to play for high stakes. Almost all teams were six-handed because this was a long, grueling event and being six-handed allowed pairs some time to rest.

It was decided that George and Eddie would sit out the matches during the search for Edith, and the other four players would continue in the event. Of course, Eddie Wold is a world-class player and while George can play, certainly the team was much stronger playing four handed, rest or no rest. Remember, this was almost 50 years ago and these guys were young and fearless.

My team was also a top seed but in the other half of the draw. This meant that if both of the two teams kept winning, we would not meet until the final. My team was playing five-handed. Alan Sontag and Sion played full time and I was rotating with Chazen and Cokin.

Where was Edith? Was there a ransom note? George was in seclusion with the FBI and the matches were continuing. Both George's team and my team had reached the quarterfinals. There were a lot of great players.

Four quarterfinal matches remained. In our half of the draw, Kathie Wei's powerhouse woman's team, consisting of Judi Radin, Jacqui Mitchell, Gail Moss, Carol Sanders and Betty Ann Kennedy lost to Ted Horning's team, John Carruthers, Pat Shorr, and Susan Handelman by 76 IMPs. We beat Jim Looby, Bill Pettis, Eugene O'Neill and Vic Chernoff by 56 IMPs.

In the other half, Rosenkrantz's team beat Harris by 21 IMPs and Brian Glubock, playing with Ron Lebensold, Jay Merrill, and Lou Reich defeated Jim Chew playing with Jim Jacoby, Al Childs, Larry Sealy, and Ron Smith by 14 IMPs.

It was Friday night and, miracle of miracles, Edith was back, safe and sound! Everyone was ecstatically happy for her and George. But now came a sticky question. Should or did George have to return to play? Was he too emotionally drained from the events of the week? His four powerhouse teammates were, of course, doing fine without him. The opponents all, of course, wanted George back in.

In those days, there was no U.S. Bridge Federation. Qualification for the Bermuda Bowl was decided in a playoff between the winners of the four major events: the Vanderbilt, the Spingold, the Reisinger, and the Grand National Teams. A decision was made: George could sit out the semifinal, (and finals if they won), but could then rejoin his team for the Bermuda Bowl qualification playoff if his team won the Spingold.

What? Seriously? Yup. OK, it was what it was. You be the judge.

But more bizarre things were on the horizon. In the semifinals, neither match was close. We won 275–89 and George's (non-George) team won 235–86.

It was to be us against the big four on Sunday. Little did we know it would end, as Alan Truscott said, in "a scenario no fiction-writer would venture."

The final stayed close, but we were always slightly trailing. I played the first half and held my own, considering I was still a "novice," playing four of the top players in the world with lots of spectators. Most of the crowd was cheering for George's, non-George, team, feeling sympathy, as we all did, for his difficult week. We trailed at halftime 87–51 and after three quarters by 117–94. It was still up for grabs.

At about 1 a.m., one table had completed play. Bergen and Cohen who had played great all week had a bad last quarter. Their misfortunes included a misdefense that allowed a game to make on a deal they themselves could have made a slam. They estimated they had lost 40 IMPs at their table.

Play was slow at the other table, finishing around 2:30. Meckstroth and Rodwell had had a good set and after about two minutes to compare scores, we had lost by four IMPs. Or had we?

A bizarre twist was to follow. It was discovered that one deal had been misduplicated by the officials; the North and East hands had been interchanged! Now what? George's team had lost 15 IMPs on the board, but now an extra board had to be played. The famous Deal No. 65! Never before and never again.

So just before 4 a.m., the players sat down. We needed to win 19 IMPs on the board to catch them. This meant that the total gross score had to be 2,000 points. This was highly improbable but accounts for the optimism you will see in the bidding. George's team, of course, was hoping for a nice quiet 1NT–3NT deal. We, on the other hand, had other thoughts.

Here is the famous Deal 65:

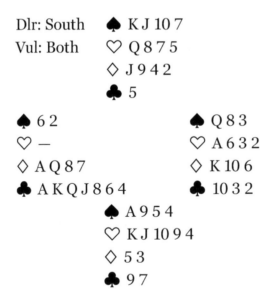

Dlr: South
Vul: Both

North
♠ K J 10 7
♡ Q 8 7 5
♢ J 9 4 2
♣ 5

West
♠ 6 2
♡ —
♢ A Q 8 7
♣ A K Q J 8 6 4

East
♠ Q 8 3
♡ A 6 3 2
♢ K 10 6
♣ 10 3 2

South
♠ A 9 5 4
♡ K J 10 9 4
♢ 5 3
♣ 9 7

Table One

West	North	East	South
Bergen	Sion	Cohen	Sontag
			4♡
5♣	6♡	Dbl	Redbl
All Pass			

The result was down four. At the other table:

West	North	East	South
Chazen	Rodwell	Cokin	Meckstroth
			Pass
7♣	All Pass		

Chazen would have made 12 tricks without a spade lead but went down two. The desired swing went in the direction of George's team.

I mentioned earlier every time I run into Larry, he brings up this hand, like I really want to hear about it. Recently, Vickie and I were on a cruise, and Larry was conducting one of his excellent weekly cruise seminars. Of course, when I popped in to say hello, he stopped what he was doing, introduced me, and went thru the whole story with his 90 students. Maybe one time he will change the ending.

SUMMER NORTH AMERICAN CHAMPIONSHIPS
Washington, D.C.
1984
The

Left to Right
Steve Sion, Alan Sontag, Dr J
Bernie Chazen, Allan Cokin

SPINGOLD MASTER KNOCKOUT TEAMS

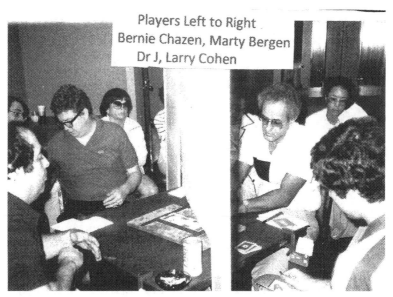

Players Left to Right
Bernie Chazen, Marty Bergen
Dr J, Larry Cohen

*Pictured above is my team from the famous (infamous) 1984 Spingold.
We did well, reaching the finals, where we lost to a really good team.*

*The Meckstroth-Rodwell and Bergen-Cohen partnerships
seen below were in their early stages.*

From Left to Right, 1984
Bergen, Meckstroth,
Rodwell. Cohen, and Wold

CHAPTER FOURTEEN
THE '90S

I had pretty much stopped playing bridge in the late 1980s. Our radiology practice had opened a chain of MRI centers covering the eastern half of the country. I was busy traveling to the centers and playing only occasionally. In November 1988, I met Marsha May, who was working as the editor of the National Enquirer based in Lantana, Florida. It was love at first sight. We even had the same birthday and we were married a year later. She wanted to learn bridge because it was a big part of my life, and she felt she needed to at least understand the "table talk."

Marsha and Jim

Well, that was easy. "I think I can arrange that," I said. Cokin and Chazen gave her lessons, and she was quickly into tournaments. Her other favorite partners were Geoff Hampson and Curtis Cheek who were just beginning to make names for themselves. Every once in awhile, they let me play on the team.

Left to Right
Jim, Marsha, Curtis Cheek
Geoff Hampson, Allan Cokin

One of my most nervous moments in bridge was in 1997. We were playing in a Swiss team event. It was the last match and the winner would win the event. If we won, Marsha would become a Life Master. And who was I playing against? Hall of Famer Paul Soloway. Great, just what I needed. But somehow we pulled it off. Geez, talk about pressure!

I began to study Italian in the early '90s and developed a love of Italy. This may have been started when we went to play in the 24th Festivale Internazionale di Bridge, a huge Swiss team event held at the Lido outside Venice. My teammates were Cokin, Marinesa Letizia, and the famous 'Doughboy Brothers', Jerry and Dennis Clerkin. Marsha, of course, came along to enjoy the trip and watch the matches. After the first day, we were in last position of sixty teams, but as the event progressed over the next few days, we never lost another match. The format was slightly different than in North America. You often played the same team more than once. Scored by Victory Points, # 1 kept playing # 2, # 3 played # 4 and so on. The biggest problem was getting Jerry and Dennis out of the great trattoria near our hotel. But somehow we finished first! As you will see in the photo, our trophy looked like the leaning tower of Pisa.

Benito Garozzo and Lea DuPont lived nearby in Palm Beach, and we enjoyed many evenings having dinner and bridge in their apartment.

I went with Benito to a bridge camp he was conducting in Italy one summer. We played golf in the morning. He was a terrible golfer which was OK, but he was slow. Suddenly around the 16th and 17th holes, he started playing faster and faster.

"Benito," I asked, "Perque hai tanta fretta?" which means, "What's the hurry?"

"Giacomo," (Jim in Italian) he replied, "They are going to run out of the eggplant parmigiana for lunch."

There would be a duplicate at night and everyone of the hundred or so players would put their names in a bowl. Benito would draw out a name to be his partner. The first night, he pulls out a slip and looks around with a straight face. "Who is James Sternberg?" The next night of course, again with a hidden slip in hand, it was Marsha.

We had a party at Lea's apartment to celebrate when Benito became a United States citizen. "Giacomo," he said, "The countries are just trading. You are becoming an Italian." Lots of good memories; her early passing was very sad.

Players Left to Right
Marsha, Jim,
Benito Garozzo, Allan Cokin

Marsha and I went on a cruise on an Italian ship one summer and ended up playing bridge most evenings with the captain. We didn't think much about it until Alan Truscott wrote his story about giving Sam Stayman's induction speech into the Bridge Hall of Fame. In his induction speech, it seems Sam and Tubby Stayman were on the same ship a few years later. And somehow the captain got them to play bridge. But before starting, he said to Stayman in his heavy Italian accent, "Before we'a start, I only plays'a two conventions: Blackwood and Sternberg." Truscott said, "So Stayman played Sternberg all week! Geez, of all the people to get confused and say this to.

A fun week – Lower left George Mittelman and Chuck Burger
In 1999 in Boston at the Fall NABC, I won my second national
championship when we won the Senior Knockout.

44

Left to Right
Billy Eisenberg, Rich Reisig, Dr J
Allan Cokin, Bob Lipsitz, Bernie Chazen

*My teammates when we won the Senior Knockout 1999.
In 2000, we would finish second to the same team
we had beaten in the finals in 1999.*

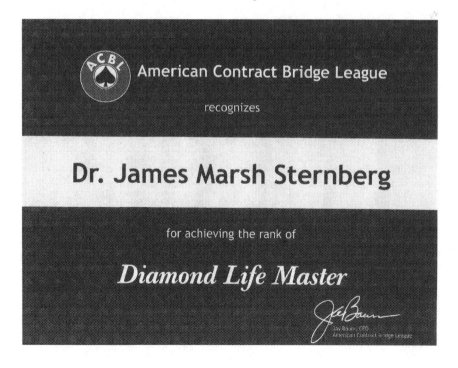

American Contract Bridge League

recognizes

Dr. James Marsh Sternberg

for achieving the rank of

Diamond Life Master

Jay Baum, CEO
American Contract Bridge League

CHAPTER FIFTEEN
THE TRAGIC YEAR

In the summer of 2001, in perfect health and perfect condition, and having never smoked, Marsha was diagnosed (by me) with lung cancer and passed away in six weeks. She was so popular in the bridge world a petition was signed by 30 of the top professionals, and the ACBL renamed the Woman's Board-A-Match National Championship. From 2002 until the event ended in 2019, it was the Marsha May Sternberg Woman's Board-A-Match. I donated and presented the trophy at every Fall NABC.

Here is the tribute which appeared in the Daily Bulletin:

Women's BAM Trophy to honor Marsha Sternberg

September 2002

Marsha Sternberg was a woman of many talents who was struck down by cancer suddenly last year. Her husband, Jim Sternberg of West Palm Beach FL, is honoring her memory by donating a trophy for the Women's Board-a- Match Teams, an event that takes place at the Fall NABC. The trophy will be known as the Marsha Sternberg Memorial Trophy. Each member of the winning team will receive a replica of the trophy. The Board of Directors has given its approval for the new award. Marsha was outstanding in many fields – she was a sailing instructor and she was very successful in golf, tennis and of course bridge. She took up the game and joined ACBL in 1990 and became a Life Master in 1997. She won many regional championships. She also was an excellent pianist.

But it was in the publishing business that she really stood out. She became the first female editor for the National Enquirer, and she climbed the ladder until she became senior editor. She became the highest paid female editor in the world. She wrote a much-read column entitled "Tales of Courage" which profiled people facing crises. She left her post at the Enquirer in 1989 when she married Jim, a radiologist. It still brings tears to Jim's eyes when he remembers viewing Marsha's x-rays and discovering that the cancer he saw had to have a fatal outcome. Marsha was a countess – the Countess of Abruzzi. This title was given to her in recognition of the couple's philanthropic efforts in Italy. One of Sternberg's favorite memories of his late wife occurred during the world championships in Albuquerque in 1994. "I had lost in the Rosenblum quarterfinals and had gone to sleep. When I woke up, there was a trophy on the table in our hotel room. I asked, "Marsha, did I win something?" "No", she said, "I won something - the novice swiss."

Sternberg's Requiem

Women's Board-a-Match trophy will honor Marsha Sternberg

PHOENIX NABC FALL 2002

Sunday, December 1

Friday–Saturday–Sunday AM Side Game Series (continue
* Stratified 299er Pairs
* Stratified 299er Swiss Teams
Stratified Fast Open Pairs
Stratified Senior Swiss Teams
OPEN BOARD-A-MATCH TEAMS
MARSHA STERNBERG WOMEN'S BOARD-A-MATCH TE
Both: 2 qualifying & 2 final sessions.

Marsha Sternberg was a woman of many talents who was struck down by cancer last year at the age of 52. Her husband, Jim Sternberg of West Palm Beach FL, is honoring her memory by donating a trophy for the Women's Board-a-Match Teams, an event that takes place at the Fall North American Bridge Championships.

The trophy will be known as the Marsha Sternberg Memorial Trophy. Each member of the winning team will receive a replica of the trophy. The ACBL Board of Directors has given its approval for the new award.

The previous trophy for this event was the Coffin Trophy, named in honor of bridge author George Coffin. The Coffin

Trophy will be retired.

Marsha Sternberg was outstanding in many fields — she was an excellent pianist and a sailing instructor. She also was very successful in golf, tennis and of course bridge. She took up the game and joined the ACBL in 1990 and became a Life Master in 1997. She won many regional championships.

It was in the publishing business that Sternberg really stood out. She became the first female editor for the National Enquirer and climbed the ladder until she became senior editor. She became the highest-paid female editor in the world.

The first Marsha Sternberg Women's Board-a-Match Teams will take place at the Phoenix NABC this fall. ☐

CHAPTER SIXTEEN
IMPROVING ONE'S GAME

So how can one get to be a better bridge player? Did you ever read the book chosen as the No. 1 bridge book of all time according to a 1994 ACBL book survey? It's called "Why You Lose at Bridge" by S.J. Simon, written in 1946. Let me quote from the introduction:

There are two primary reasons [why you lose]: a) lack of technical skill, and b) losing tactics. It is not the object of this book to do much about the first. It is probably too late to do much about it anyhow. You've been playing bridge far too long now to start learning how to play your dummy better ... you've been making the same mistakes quite happily for years and you've every intention to go on making them. You don't want to know how to make a contract on a double squeeze, dummy reversal, or throw-in.

And quite right, too. I sympathize. Bridge is a game and you play it for pleasure ... leave such highly technical plays to the expert ... it's not the handling of difficult hands that makes the winning player. There aren't enough of them. It's the ability to avoid messing up the easy ones.

Your technique is good enough to make you a winning player. But you're not ... and now I'll wait while you tell me you play bridge for pleasure and don't care if you win or lose as long as you enjoy the game. But I have yet to meet the 'I play for pleasure' person who gets up after a losing session looking pleased. Let us be cold-blooded about this. We all play bridge to win ... so let us ... be frank with each other. After all, you don't have to admit to anyone else that you agree with me ... you would rather win. Right. Now we can get on.

So what's holding us back from improving? S.J. Simon says that it's losing tactics, but I think I can add one more later.

Tactics. Have you ever read the book by Fred Karpin "Psychological Strategy in Contract Bridge"? This was published in 1960 with a subtitle of "The Techniques of

Deception and Harassment in Bidding and Play." Let me quote from Chapter One titled "The Necessity for Deception and Obstructive Bidding Tactics":

... thru the years, the attention has been paid to the problems of those who 'have', the 'have-nots' have become the forgotten generation. But then measures began to be introduced for the benefit of the 'have-nots'. Weak two-bids, weak jump overcalls and responses, preempts, psychs, etc., ... no expert tries to play an absolutely sound 'book' game ... he must try to push the opponents into making mistakes.

And this thinking dates back to 1960. Yet I see so many players who are stereotyped 'book' players and expect to get maximum mileage out of their good or bad cards. Making a contract by misleading or tricking the opponents counts just as much as by brute force. On defense, preventing them from finding their proper contract counts the same as defeating a contract by highly skilled play.

Karpin points out that properly applied harassment and deception will also introduce color and zest into the game. He points out that bridge would be a dull game if all bidding proceeded along strict mathematical lines and rules. "Partner, you need X number of points for this, and Z number of points for that," etc. As Bernie Chazen often pointed out, point-counters never learn to become bridge players.

For example, what would you open with the following two hands:

(A) ♠A J 10 9 ♡K J 9 ♢Q 10 9 ♣Q J 7
(B) ♠A 8 5 4 ♡K J 4 ♢K 7 3 ♣A 6 3
Hand (A) has 14 HCP while hand (B) has 15 HCP.

A point-counter would open (A) 1♣ and (B) 1NT. I certainly believe any bridge player would do just the reverse. The chunky hand (A) is much better than (B).

If your partner opened 1♢, what would you bid with:

(A) ♠K Q 8 5 2 ♡8 7 6 ♢6 ♣ 10 6 5 4
(B) ♠Q 4 3 2 ♡Q 6 3 ♢7 2 ♣Q 5 3 2

I saw the same person pass hand (A) but gladly bid 1♠ on (B) because hand (A) had 5 HCP while (B) had 6 HCP. I suggested this might not be the game for her. I received a quizzical look.

Weak two-bids with strong five-card suits, off-shape preempts or weak jump overcalls? If you never leave the "book," you are missing a lot. Karpin closes Chapter One by writing "... by studying the expert approach ... and applying some of their strategy, you will derive more enjoyment of the game ..."

The modern style is not to pass partner's opening bid with the slightest excuse for responding. In the September 2005 issue of the Bridge Bulletin, someone asked Eric Kokish, one of the finest coaches in the game: "Recently, you mentioned that you liked to respond very light. *How* light?"

Eric's reply was this: "There are no hands with a five-card major that I would pass in response to 1♣ or 1◇, and most 3- or 4-counts are clear-cut responses ... I would never pass 1♡ or 1♠ with support or shortness."

From The Bridge World bidding contest, May 2011. North deals, E–W vulnerable:

West	East
♠ K 6 3	♠ A J 7 5
♡ J 5 3	♡ A K Q 9
◇ J 9 4 2	◇ A K 8 7
♣ 10 3 2	♣ 7

Fleisher	Kamil
	1◇
Pass	

Smith	Cohen
	1◇
1NT	2♠
3◇	3♡
4◇	5◇
Pass	

The Bridge World Standard auction was the one by Smith–Cohen.

From the Bermuda Bowl in 2007:

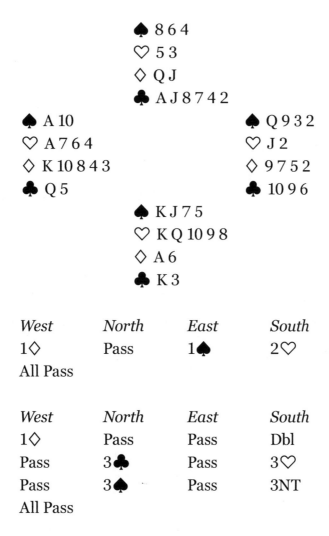

♠ 8 6 4
♡ 5 3
◇ Q J
♣ A J 8 7 4 2

♠ A 10
♡ A 7 6 4
◇ K 10 8 4 3
♣ Q 5

♠ Q 9 3 2
♡ J 2
◇ 9 7 5 2
♣ 10 9 6

♠ K J 7 5
♡ K Q 10 9 8
◇ A 6
♣ K 3

West	North	East	South
1◇	Pass	1♠	2♡
All Pass			

West	North	East	South
1◇	Pass	Pass	Dbl
Pass	3♣	Pass	3♡
Pass	3♠	Pass	3NT
All Pass			

Notice how at the first table, East, Steve Garner for the USA, responded to Howie Weinstein's opening bid. At the other table, East passed and Zia and Michael Rosenberg had no trouble reaching 3NT. That was 8 IMPs to USA over Norway.

Bridge is very much like golf and tennis. Let's look at some of the psychological factors affecting your bridge game and compare them to say, tennis. An article in "Tennis", January/February 2011, called "5 minutes with Nick" by the great tennis coach Nick Bolliteri, asks "What does it take to win on a court?" How can we relate this to bridge? Well, let's see.

Be steady. Most people say they need a bigger serve or harder forehand. That would be nice, but they are not the most important tools. What you need is consistency. Unforced errors lose matches. Don't believe me? Pull up the stats of any match and see for yourself. It's rare when a player commits more errors and wins the match. Likewise in bridge, making the unforced errors. You don't have to "hit" the double squeeze; you do have to make 3NT when you are supposed to.

Get in better physical shape. Winning takes patience. If you are carrying a few extra pounds, staying in there at the end may be difficult. It's the same in bridge. Endurance. Being alert and sharp at the end when others are tired. More matches are won at the end when others are bored or tired. Don't eat a big meal before playing.

Do what you do best. In tennis if you are down 30–40, if your serve is your strength, don't take a little off because it's a tight position. If you are a good preemptor, or have good table feel, go with your strong points.

Play, don't pray. Make things happen rather than hope your opponent misses. Yes, unforced errors lose matches, but if you just stand there hitting weak shots hoping your opponent will miss, it's a losing way to play. That's why preempting pays off. Move them out of their comfort zone.

And finally, Nick says, have an attitude. All physical skills being equal, you need a mental edge. Same in bridge: Act like a winner. Forget the last hand. Every hand, just like every point, is a new opportunity and can be won!

What about tactics? What about the difference between matchpoints and IMPs? Yes, we all know about in team games with IMP scoring about stretching to bid vulnerable games, ignoring tiny swings, and selling out on partscore deals. But have you ever considered the objectives of the two games?

In a classic article, written many years ago by then-Bridge World editor Edgar Kaplan, he pointed out that at matchpoints, you are trying to beat a large number of pairs. In a large field, there will be many weaker or less-experienced pairs. At IMPs, you are trying to beat one team (at a time). A 51% game wins a team game. A 51% game at pairs leaves you in the middle of the field. So in a team game, playing down the middle, taking what is yours, not trying to steal what belongs to the enemy and just making few mistakes almost always wins the match. Playing this way in pairs will be a disaster; often, even a 61% game is not enough. You must take more chances, more "bad" actions, to win pair games.

As an example, Kaplan showed this hand:

♠6　　♡K Q 10 8 6 4　　◇A J 10 6 3　　♣2.

He noted that at pairs he would open 4♡, while in a team game he would want better heart spots to protect against any disaster. He would also worry that he might belong in diamonds. He would open 1♡, going slow, to see what he could actually make.

He noted that when playing in a pair game against Al Roth, founder of the sound Roth-Stone system, that he could hardly remember playing a set of two boards in which Roth did not make some unusual or unsound bid: a preempt; an unusual balance; a "position;" a normal game played in a partscore, or the like. But in a team game, Roth was a solid, conservative citizen.

Do you play golf or tennis? Do you take lessons? Do you spend a lot on the latest equipment? Expensive greens fees? Yes, of course you do. How much have you spent (invested) in your bridge game? Probably nothing, yet you spend a lot of time at the bridge table. From my own experience coaching, 95% of folks who seek help are women. Why? Ego, of course, but I can tell you from observations over many years, there is no sex difference in the degree of how badly one plays bridge.

If you want to get better, you have to stop playing in Flight X and move up to play with better players. Sure, you will take a beating for awhile, but you will only get better. You need to play against and with better players or you will never be aware of your errors. You need to take playing lessons with good coaches. Stop thinking about masterpoints!

CHAPTER SEVENTEEN
EPILOGUE

After the untimely passing of my wife Marsha in 2001, I stopped playing much bridge except for an occasional event, but did a lot of coaching. In 2008 and 2009, I was the coach for the United States Junior Teams, USA Blue and USA Red. They had qualified at the USBF Junior Team Trials to go to Istanbul, Turkey to play in the World Bridge Federation World Youth Championships.

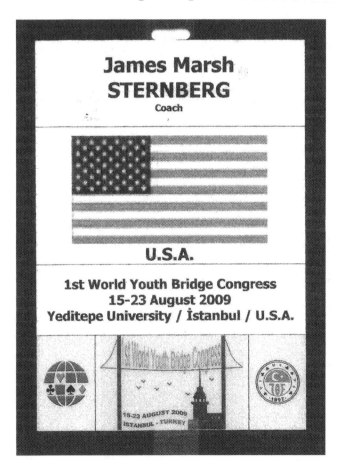

The USA Blue Team took home a bronze medal in Turkey: Kevin Fay, Justin Lall, Jeremy Fournier, Matt Meckstroth (front), npc Howard Weinstein (back), Jason Chiu, Kevin Dwyer and coach Jim Sternberg.

The USA Red Team also scored a bronze medal: Adam Kaplan, Alex Hudson, Zach Brescoll, Cameron Shunta, Owen Lien, coach Sternberg, John Marriott and npc Weinstein.

The Coach and The 'Kids"

USBF

UNITED STATES BRIDGE FEDERATION
"SERVING THE BRIDGE ATHLETES OF THE USA"

February 14, 2006

Dr. James Sternberg
1808 Breakers West Blvd.
West Palm Beach FL 33411-5116

Dear Jim:

Thank you very much for your generous contribution to the United States Bridge Federation given to specifically support the United States Junior Bridge Program. This donation will help make it possible for the USBF to send two teams to represent the United States in the 2006 World Schools Team Championship in Thailand.

Also, thank you for agreeing to be the Schools Teams coach and working with them to improve their bridge. I know that it takes a lot of time and effort to coordinate practice sessions and discuss strategy with them.

Junior bridge is very important to the future of the game. The USBF and I sincerely appreciate your support.

Sincerely,

Charlotte Blaiss

Charlotte Blaiss
Director of Youth Programs
Charlotte.blaiss@acbl.org

We were all meeting at JFK airport. Our non-playing captain Howie Weinstein had already made his first good decision. He would go a day later leaving me to worry about the "kids." Of course, as soon as I arrived at JFK, my cell phone started ringing. Adam Kaplan, being only thirteen years old was an unaccompanied minor so he couldn't check in. I had to go back out, get him and re-enter. The next call was Owen Lien; his plane coming from Atlanta was going to be three hours late. Great! We hadn't even begun. When we were finally ready to leave, I was missing five players. Two got in as they were closing the plane door. Owen got re-routed through Paris and the others arrived a day late.

There were 40 teams with a three-day Swiss, with eight teams to qualify for the Knock-Out phase. USA Blue went 13-0 while USA Red finished fourteenth. The non-qualifiers would enter a Board-A-Match consolation. USA Blue, feeling unbeatable, choose Greece for it's quarterfinal match and destroyed them by ONE imp! Then they continued their fine performance by losing to Italy in the semi-finals 72-45. The next day would be a play-off for third place and the Bronze medal against the Netherlands.

Down 27-0 after 3 boards, 27 at halftime, and still down 14 after three quarters, the team rallied to be tied when they got to the last board.

DLR East	♠ 108643		West	North	East	South
Vul None	♡ A		Meckstroth		Dwyer	
	◇ AJ2				P	P
	♣ J1076		1♡	Dbl	3◇	4♣
♠ A752		♠ QJ9	4♡	P	P	Dbl
♡ QJ10762		♡ K983				
◇ 3		◇ Q10754	3◇ was a fit-showing bid. North led a			
♣ A3		♣ 9	spade, later gave his partner a ruff for			
	♠ K		down one, -100			
	♡ 54					
	◇ K986					
	♣ KQ8542					

At the other table:

West	North	East	South
	Lall		Fournier
		P	2♣ (Precision)
2♡	3♡	4♡	P
P	5♣	Dbl	All Pass

West led her singleton diamond but East had no entry to give partner a ruff. The spades were 4-3 so declarer could discard diamond losers later on the spades. +550, +10 IMP's and a Bronze medal!

Meanwhile in the consolation Board-A-Match, USA Red after a slow start, had a big finish to win the Bronze medal.

Kevin Fay's play on this hand was a big factor:

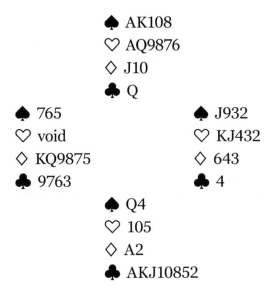

The opponents bid and made 6♣. Kevin Fay and Jason Chiu reached 7♡ (please don't ask about the bidding) which was 'loudly' doubled by East, a good example of don't double the only contract you can beat.

While Fay was on the opposite side of the screen, he believed his opponent and ran to 7NT. After the lead of the ◇K, he unblocked the ♡A, and ran the clubs to reach this position:

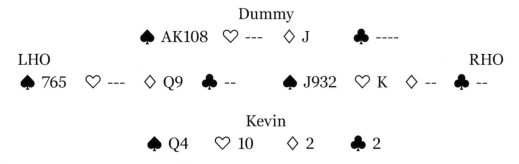

When declarer led his last club, if LHO had 4 spades and the ◇Q, he would have been squeezed. When the ◇Q did not appear, Fay pitched the ◇J from dummy. Now RHO was squeezed. If he threw a heart, the ♡ 10 was high. If he threw a spade, the spades were good. Nice going Kevin!

After 12 long days it was time to come home. No one had lost their passport and we all got to the airport on time. Everyone came home with a medal. Special thanks to Jan Martel and Barbara Nudelman for their efforts.

This was really a terrific experience. You might recognize some of the 'kids' who are more well known now in adult bridge circles. Sadly Justin Lall passed away at a young age.

Fred Hamilton and I played in a few national events. In 2006, playing in the Senior Pairs, this hand was in the Daily Bulletin. I had published a brief article in Bridge World suggesting adding a slight twist to the Kokish Relay. That convention, invented by Eric Kokish, avoids having to jump to 3NT after a 2♣–2◊ auction with extras by using 2♡ as a relay to 2♠, then 2NT being forcing.

If playing controls, Ace=2 and King= 1, then after a 2♣ opening, 2♡ is a frequent response. This is usually not a problem because opener can bid 2NT, knowing partner is unlikely to pass. I invented the idea of using 2♠ after a 2♡ reply to say "I was going to 'Kokish' if you had bid 2◊. Please treat my 2♠ bid as a forcing 2NT bid with all systems on."

This hand came up:

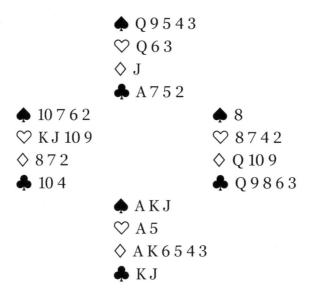

North	South
Fred	Dr. J
	2♣
2♡(1)	2♠(2)
3♡(3)	3♠
4♣(4)	4◇(4)
4♠	4NT(5)
5♣(6)	5◇(7)
5NT(8)	6◇(9)
6NT(10)	7♠
Pass	

(1) One ace or two kings

(2) Spades or 24-plus HCP, balanced

(3) Transfer to spades as if partner had bid notrump

(4) Cue bids

(5) Roman Keycard Blackwood (knowing the answer, but planning to ask for the ♠Q)

(6) One keycard

(7) Do you have the trump queen?

(8) Yes, and pick a slam

(9) Do you have help in diamonds?

(10) Yes, and something extra (the ♡Q and ◇J)

Even though the spade suit didn't split, the grand slam still made because diamonds were 3–3 and West couldn't profitably lead a heart.

We didn't win the event that year, but in 2012, we did win the same event, the Senior Pairs (Leventritt Silver Ribbon Pairs).

Silver Ribbon champs: Fred Hamilton and James Marsh Sternberg

Hamilton, Sternberg win Silver Ribbon Pairs

James Marsh Sternberg and Fred Hamilton captured **first place** in the **Leventritt Silver Ribbon Pairs**, capitalizing on a huge score in the first final session. Sternberg and Hamilton won the four session contest by more than two boards. **Sternberg, a three-time NABC winner**, and Hamilton, a Hall of Fame member, two-time world champion and 16-time NABC champ, qualified in the middle of the field after Sunday's opening round, but posted a blistering 71.18% in the first final to take the lead. Their second session score of 58.79% gave the winners a total of 2725.44 (top was 77).

In that event, I had the best round of bridge I have ever had. We qualified in the upper half, but the first final was incredible. It was one good board after another.

Talk about being in a zone. Could we have a nice quiet last board? Of course not:

♠ Q 10 7 6 5
♡ A Q 10
◇ 5
♣ J 10 5 2

♠ —
♡ K 5 3
◇ A K Q 7 2
♣ A K Q 8 7

North	South
Fred	*Dr. J*
	1◇
1♠ (1)	3♣
3♡ (2)	3NT
4♣ (3)	4◇ (3)
4NT (4)	7♣ (5)
Pass	

(1) Of course! Big help

(2) Cue bid or try for 3NT

(3) Cue bid, as was 3♡

(4) Too good for 5♣, but nothing else to say

(5) Why not? Everything had been going our way.

If you have ever played with Freddy, you will understand what I mean next: His looks can kill. Obviously, he knew we were having a big game.

When the opening leader tabled the ♠A, the look on Freddy's face defied description. When I ruffed it, for plus 2140 and 75/77 of the matchpoints, there was a nice smile. We had a little over 71% in a national pair game, unheard of. It was a set for the ages. A 60%+ game in the evening sealed the deal.

A WILD RIDE IN THE SILVER RIBBON PAIRS
Reprinted from Florida Sunshine Bridge News, May 2012

71%+ in a national pair game? You got to be kidding. We would have taken 60% and run for the door. 70% scores are sometimes seen at your local duplicate, but in a national event where a pair of 60% games in the final would usually run away with the event?

I had gone to the Spring NABC in Memphis only to play in the Silver Ribbon Pairs, the Senior Open, a four-session event with Fred Hamilton. The first day, we qualified somewhere in the middle of the field. The fireworks started immediately on the second day.

When the Daily Bulletin asked us if there were any hands that stood out, we didn't know where to begin. Of course we had some help.

The action started on the first round. I had, non-vul against vul, Bd. 6:

♠10   ♡—   ◇A K 7 6 3   ♣K Q 10 7 6 5 4,

and RHO opened 1♡. I bid 2♣. It went 4♣ on my left, 5♣ by Freddy, 5♡ on my right.

I "saved" in 6♣ which LHO doubled. Fred had:

♠J 9 7 6 5 4   ♡10   ◇10   ♣A J 9 8 3.

+1090 was 72/77 matchpoints. 77 was top on a board.

On the second round, when the opponents saved on both boards and we were +800 and +1100 for two 77s, it felt like a good beginning. But, of course, I couldn't stand prosperity. On the next two boards (Nos. 10 & 11), I reverted to my old "go low" habit and got us our only two below-average results.

I opened 1♠ with:

♠K Q 10 8 7 6   ♡K 2   ◇A 5 2   ♣K 2.

LHO bid 2♡, Fred raised to 2♠, RHO bid 3♡. Since there was no room, double would be a maximal double, a game try but I only bid 3♠, to play, not invitational. Fred had:

♠J 9 4   ♡Q 5   ◇K J 9 8 4 3   ♣10 6.

Not a great game, but LHO made the normal lead of his singleton ◇10! Holding all three aces, LHO could never get RHO in. Making four was worth only 20/77.

Even worse was the next. I had:

♠A Q 10 8 5 3   ♡A   ◇10 9 7   ♣A 10 7.

I opened 1♠. 3◇ by LHO. 3♠ by Fred, and I passed. Opposite:

♠K J 4   ♡Q J 10 7   ◇8   ♣9 8 6 5 4,

I easily made five with a ruffing finesse in hearts. +200 was worth a whopping 15/77. Freddy gave me one of his famous looks that makes you want to crawl under the table. Since I didn't want to see that again, that was our last board below 40%.

Bd. 14 was a classic example of why you should play that bidding RHO's suit in a response to a takeout double should be natural. The bidding proceeded as follows:

Me	LHO	Fred	RHO
1♣	Dbl	1♡	Pass
2♣	Pass	3♣	All Pass

Fred had stolen the board. The full deal:

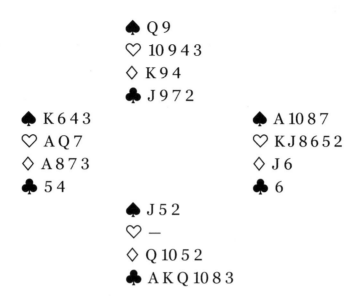

♠ Q 9
♡ 10 9 4 3
◇ K 9 4
♣ J 9 7 2

♠ K 6 4 3
♡ A Q 7
◇ A 8 7 3
♣ 5 4

♠ A 10 8 7
♡ K J 8 6 5 2
◇ J 6
♣ 6

♠ J 5 2
♡ —
◇ Q 10 5 2
♣ A K Q 10 8 3

RHO had passed throughout the auction, cold for 4♡, while I scored +130 in 3♣.
After the round at the table, Fred said, "I was hoping you couldn't (wouldn't) bid over 3♣." That was worth 72/77.

Then came Bd. 17, no one vul.
Freddy opened 4♣, and your RHO bid 4♡. You bid 4♠. LHO bid 5♡, Freddy doubled, and we collected +100 for 75/77.
Fred had:

♠7   ♡5   ◇9 6 2   ♣A Q 9 8 7 6 5 3,

and I had:

♠A K Q 9 5 4 3   ♡J   ◇8 5 3   ♣10 2.

We scored two spades and one club.

We got very lucky on Bd. 21. I opened 1◇ with:

♠A K 10 3   ♡J   ◇Q J 7 5 2   ♣K J 4.

Freddy had:

♠—   ♡3 2   ◇K 10 8 6 4   ♣A 10 9 8 6 3.

LHO bid 2◇ for the majors. When the smoke cleared and everyone stopped bidding, I was in 6◇, but they led a spade and +1370 was all the matchpoints.

OK, two rounds to go. I just wanted to get back to the barn, hoping for nothing bad to happen, knowing we were doing pretty good. Who knew how good? I hoped Fred could just play a few 1NTs or something and finish up. But no:

Four more wild boards were coming. Little did I know we were about to score 76, 62, 67 and 75 on the last four boards!

Bd. 25: At favorable, Fred opened 3◇ with:

♠4   ♡10   ◇A J 8 7 6 4   ♣K 9 8 7 3

and bought the contract, scoring +130 while they were cold for 4♡ or 4♠.

Bd. 26: I opened 2NT with:

♠A K 8   ♡A 10 9   ◇A Q J 8   ♣Q 10 8.

Fred transferred to spades and bid 5NT, pick a slam, holding:

♠10 9 7 5 2   ♡K Q 4   ◇K   ♣A 7 5 2.

Naturally, I pigged it up with 6NT. They led a diamond, and spades were 3–2, so we were +1440 for 62/77.

Finally, the last round. On the first board, Fred had:

♠K 9 5 3   ♡—   ◇A 10 3   ♣J 8 7 6 5 4.

He passed, it went 2♡ on his left, Pass–Pass back to him. Would you double or pass? He doubled! Opener had a good weak two-bid, including ♡K Q 9 7 4 3, but I had:

♠A 2   ♡A J 10 8 5   ◇K 9 4   ♣10 3 2

for +500 and 67/77 matchpoints.

A quiet last board? (Note- discussed earlier) Of course not; I get dealt:

♠—   ♡K 5 3   ◇A K Q 7 2   ♣A K Q 8 7.

Great. So I opened 1◇, Fred bid 1♠ (of course). I bid 3♣, he bid 3♡, I tried 3NT, and he bid 4♣. So his 3♡ was a cuebid for clubs. OK, 4♣ and his next bid, 4NT, was DI, saying he was a little too good for 5♣ but had nothing else to say. Now what? I knew he had nothing wasted in spades from his failure to cuebid 4♠. Last board of a big set, not too important, only maybe a national championship riding on this. But things had been going well. So I bid 7♣, why not?

LHO led the ♠A, Fred nervously tabled:

♠Q 10 7 6 5   ♡A Q 10   ◇5   ♣J 10 5 2,

and I quickly was writing down +2140 for 75/77 on the final board. There were not a lot of pairs in 7♣. No kidding. Whew, a set for the ages.

That evening, when we sat down for the final session, Freddy had some very good advice. He said, "Don't worry if tonight doesn't feel like this afternoon. It can't. Just hang in, and we will do fine." It was very good advice because our evening 59%+ game felt like we were having a bad game after the afternoon session.

On the very first board, Freddy opened 1NT. I held:

♠K Q J ♡A Q 8 6 ♢10 9 6 5 ♣A 5.

So, go high, go low? I took the middle road bidding 4NT. Fred passed with:

♠A 4 ♡K 10 7 ♢K Q 7 3 2 ♣K 6 2.

Of course the ♢A J 8 was on his right and 6NT was cold. Were we off to a bad start? Turned out we got 26/77.

But the evening went very well. We defended very well, some of the hands you might have seen in the Daily Bulletin and the New York Times. I felt things were going to be OK. On the last round, we were +300 against our partial on the first board, then on the last board we bid this slam:

♠ A K 10 9 2
♡ 10 8 6 5
♢ J 9 7
♣ 2

♠ J
♡ A K Q 7
♢ A K 8 6 3
♣ 9 5 3

North	South
Fred	*Me*
	1♢
1♠	2♡
4♣(1)	4NT
5♣	6♡
Pass	

(1) Singleton club with 4+ hearts. I had to have the right hand with ♣953 opposite his singleton, so I pushed towards slam.

They cashed the ♣A on the opening lead. After drawing trumps, I finally had to play the ◇A K, and the queen fell! Some days, it's just going to be your day. 71/77 and we had won the Silver Ribbon Pairs.

In 2014, we won the silver medal in Sanya, China, losing a close final in the World Senior Team Championship.

The all-American Rand Cup Senior Team silver medal squad: Billy Eisenberg, Neil Chambers, James Marsh Sternberg (captain), John Schermer, Arnold Fisher and Fred Hamilton.

CHASING GOLD IN CHINA

From The Sunshine Bridge News, January 2015

The World Championships were held in mid-October in Sanya, China, the southernmost location in China, an hour's flight south of Hong Kong. I'm sure arranging to get there was more difficult than playing. It began by having to email a Mr. Wu in China to first get a letter of invitation, necessary for your visa, and he was in charge of making your hotel reservation. Forget trying to call the MGM Grand or the Sheraton; they don't do things that way in China, you go thru Mr. Wu. Then, after a couple of months of this, you get your letter and start your visa application.

By now, you have such a headache you are having serious second thoughts about going. And, of course, you have to email Mr. Wu a photo for your badge. And an email photo, front and back of your credit card for the hotel, all of which is charged, non-refundable, before you even get started. And then there is your plane reservation. It's easier to get to Mars than Sanya. And of course you have to be sure your teammates are getting their stuff together, too.

Fred Hamilton, one of my teammates, actually showed up at the Las Vegas airport ready to go only to find that the ticket he thought he had bought had somehow never gone thru, so he had to run home and rebook something.

Because Worldbridge falls under the auspices of the International Olympic Committee, world bridge competitions are subject to the same anti-doping regulations, and players are warned in advance by the WBF to expect random drug testing. Have you ever gone to the website where they list the banned medication? It reads like the list of every drug ever invented!

I was afraid to take an aspirin during the three months leading up to the event. Most players over 50 are on some prescribed medication. Yes, you can apply for a medical exemption, but that's like asking to be tested. And all seniors are on some prescribed medication (or unprescribed).

But in checking the fine print of the Conditions of Contest, nowhere did it mention drug testing "seniors." I wrote the WBF and asked if this was an omission and received in writing "Seniors will not be tested." The team breathed a sigh of relief!

So now, you finally get going and it takes forever. I flew to Seattle, overnighted, then a 12-hour flight to Hong Kong, a few days there to recover from the 12-hour time change, then flew to Sanya.

The MGM Grand is really a beautiful resort on the South China Sea. Still jetlagged, we started our event consisting of three days of qualifying, a round robin of seven matches each day to qualify eight teams for the knockout phase, which would be three days of 54-board matches. The order of finish in the qualifier is important because the top four get to pick their opponents from the bottom four. Number one picks first, etc. So the "death" seat is to qualify fourth: You get the team no one wanted to play. Of course, we qualified fourth. And who was left in the bottom four? Sure, the defending champs and the best team, Mike Passell, Eddie Wold, Bart Bramley, Lew Stansby and Marc Jacobus.

Great! We had to go all the way to Sanya just to play the other USA team. But we beat them in the quarterfinal, so now we had to play Paul Hackett and company from Great Britain, the team who had won the year before. Some draw we had gotten. But miracles kept coming. We won again and now we were in the finals. Wow! But by now, after two weeks, I was getting a little tired of Chinese food. The final against a mostly mixed European team was close, about even after three quarters but we didn't do well in the last quarter and ended up with the Silver medal instead of Gold.

Well, was it worth it? Sure, it was a great experience, very exciting, and we came as close to winning a world championship as possible. Of course, now came the long, long, trip home. It took one day to go from Sanya and overnight in Hong Kong, where I had a nice evening having dinner with Alan Sontag and his wife, Robin, who were staying at my hotel.

Then, the next day, Hong Kong to Seattle was strange because you leave Monday morning and arrive Monday morning, then on to Atlanta and then West Palm. Whew. That was a long day. But I can't wait to do it again.

Playing in a Swiss teams at the Fall NABC that year, you face this problem:

$$\spadesuit \text{ K 8 7 6 2}$$
$$\heartsuit \text{ A 10}$$
$$\diamond \text{ 10 4}$$
$$\clubsuit \text{ A Q 8 2}$$

$$\spadesuit \text{ A Q 9 5}$$
$$\heartsuit \text{ 7}$$
$$\diamond \text{ A K J 7 2}$$
$$\clubsuit \text{ 10 6 3}$$

West	North	East	South
3♡	Dbl	4♡	5♠
Pass	6♠	All Pass	

Opening Lead: ♣ 7

The opening lead could easily be a singleton, so you need to set up the diamonds to pitch two clubs from dummy. If diamonds are 3–3 or the ◇Q is singleton or doubleton, you are home. But, of course, diamonds are 4–2 with West having ◇Q 8 6 2. You finish down two. But look at the entire deal:

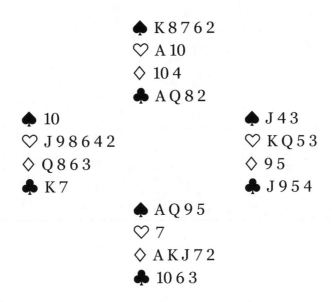

```
              ♠ K 8 7 6 2
              ♡ A 10
              ◇ 10 4
              ♣ A Q 8 2
 ♠ 10                          ♠ J 4 3
 ♡ J 9 8 6 4 2                 ♡ K Q 5 3
 ◇ Q 8 6 3                     ◇ 9 5
 ♣ K 7                         ♣ J 9 5 4
              ♠ A Q 9 5
              ♡ 7
              ◇ A K J 7 2
              ♣ 10 6 3
```

Who was that sneaky guy who led the ♣7 from ♣K 7? Nice lead, Dr. J!

At the other table, my partners stopped in 4♠ making five. Win 11 IMPs instead of losing 11. A 22-IMP swing and a first-place finish.

You can't trust anyone these days.

For a few years, I did a TV show. It was done originally for closed circuit where Vickie Bader and I live. It was a take-off on Wheel of Fortune. We had a large board with the cards and Vanna (Vickie) would walk back and forth turning cards as I was talking. I did a short monologue first, then a lesson. We had some guests, including Marty Bergen, Keith Hanson, and Michael Schaeffer.

The shows ran for a few years, but you can still see them on YouTube under Ballen Isles Bridge or on Bergen's website. Fun.

Doping in sports has become a serious issue and bridge is no exception. In 2018, the World Bridge Federation president, Gianarrigo Roma invited me to join the WBF Medical & Prevention Commission which oversees the antidoping procedures.

"Bridge for Peace"

International Sport Federation (IF) recognized by the International Olympic Committee

Gianarrigo Rona
President

Prof. James Sternberg

His address

Lausanne, 26th June 2018

Dear James, caro Giacomo,

I am very pleased to inform you that the Management Committee of the WBF at its meeting held in Ostend on 15th June unanimously approved your appointment as member of the WBF Medical & Prevention Commission.

I hope in your acceptance, being confident that we will greatly benefit from your contribution to our work.

Congratulating you on behalf of the Commission and personally, I remain at your complete disposal.

In Orlando, where other members of the Commission will be for the Antidoping procedures, we can meet and talk about the activity of the Commission.

Looking forward to meeting you,

Yours sincerely
Gianarrigo

ARISF GAISF IMSA International Mind Sports Association

Headquarters: Maison du Sport International ~ 54 av. de Rhodanie ~ 1007 Lausanne ~ Switzerland
Tel.: +41 21 544 7218 ~ Fax: +41 21 601 2315
President's Address : Via Moscova 46/5 ~ 20121 Milano ~ Italy
Tel.: +39 02 367 04 987 ~ Fax: +39 02 367 05 962
president@worldbridgefed.com

I have published many articles over the years in the Bridge Bulletin, The Bridge World and elsewhere. These were two original articles when the Bulletin had a column called the Bidding Lab, a place for writers to suggest new ideas.

Bidding Lab

Ideas and innovations from ACBL members

Art by Brian McDermott

March 2007
www.acbl.org

Fine tuning 2NT

By Dr. Jim Sternberg

Very big balanced hands (23 or more high-card points) can cause problems, especially when opener jumps to 3NT after partner's response to a 2♣ opening, necessary because after 2♣ – 2♦ (waiting, negative, whatever), a 2NT rebid is non-forcing. This results in the loss of most systemic responses such as Stayman, Jacoby transfers, whatever your agreements are.

Eric Kokish made a big contribution toward solving this by using a relay after the 2♦ response, with 2♥ by opener forcing 2♠, then 2NT being forcing and unlimited (with various other bids to show hands with hearts). Let me suggest a few further refinements.

First, I urge you to play "control responses" over a 2♣ opening. Opener needs to know yours aces and kings, not your HCP with queens and jacks. It's very easy. Aces are two controls, kings are one, so the responses to a 2♣ opener are:

2♦ = fewer than two controls (a king at most).
2♥ = two controls (an ace or two kings).
2♠ = three controls (an ace and a king, or three kings).

To avoid taking away opener's ability to rebid 2NT, I suggest the following:

1) With more than three controls, not unusual (two aces, for example), bid 2♦ over 2♣. Remember, when opener rebids 2NT, responder is the captain. It's not a problem because when opener signs off opposite your "fewer than two controls," you are not going to pass. Therefore, 2♣ – 2♦ means fewer than two controls or more than three.

2) Do not, as some recommend, use 2NT as a response to show a touching ace-king or three kings. You lose your system and don't pick up enough benefit. Just bid 2♠, showing three controls and letting opener rebid 2NT, his most common action.

3) Hands in the 20–21 range are more common than 22–23, so I reverse the common meanings: a 2NT rebid after opening 2♣ shows 20–21, while opening 2NT shows 22–23.

Another note: In playing the Kokish relay of 2♣ – 2♦; 2♥ – 2♠; 2NT shows a "good" 23 or more HCP (with a five-card suit or with lots of 10s and 9s) and is forcing with all systems on. Occasionally, partner responds 2♥ over 2♣. To retain the relay, I play that 2♣ – 2♥; 2♠ is artificial, saying I was going to "Kokish," so treat my 2♠ bid as a forcing 2NT bid. Note, however, that when opener rebids 2♠ after responder's 2♥, 2NT does not exist, but 3♣ is Stayman, 3♦ and 3♥ are Jacoby transfers, etc.

After 2♣ – 2♦, 2NT is 20–21, the "little one." You didn't open 2NT, so you can't have the middle one. If it goes 2♣ – 2♠ and you were going to "Kokish," you are forced to simply rebid 2NT, but partner has three controls, so you will keep bidding. It's less of a problem and again, partner knows your range when you, as opener, bid "one more time."

Finally, playing Kokish, when you really have the one- or two-suiter with hearts, Eric suggests that after:

2♣ – 2♦; 2♥ – 2♠,
   3♣ = clubs and hearts
   3♦ = diamonds and hearts
   3♥ = hearts.
   3♠ = hearts and spades.

I suggest interchanging the meanings of 3♣ and 3♥. The one-suiter in hearts is the more common hand type in these situations, and by having 3♣ show the one-suiter, you can use 3♦ as a double negative and stop in 3♥.

Try some of these variations. I think they will improve your 2NT openings, but please don't use them when you play against me. I have enough problems already. ❑

The author is a Diamond Life Master and two-time North American champion who lives and teaches bridge in Palm Beach Gardens FL.

Send your ideas and innovations to editor@acbl.org.

November 2009
www.acbl.org

Bidding Lab

Ideas and innovations from ACBL members

Bridge Bulletin

Raising with "only" three-card support

By Jim Stemberg

After an auction starting 1 minor – Pass – 1 major – Pass, it used to be considered almost "illegal" to raise partner's major with three-card support. But clearly there are so many hands where this is the correct action rather than a 1NT rebid. It usually depends on your holding and spot cards in the other major. For example, after partner responds 1 ♥ to my 1 ♣ opener, I would rebid 1NT with:

♠ A 8 6   ♥ K 4 3   ♦ A 10 5   ♣ K 9 4 2,

but 2 ♥ with:

♠ 7 4 2   ♥ A Q 4   ♦ A 7 4   ♣ K 8 4 3.

Holding:

♠ 7 5 3   ♥ Q 10 8   ♦ A Q 2   ♣ A J 8 7,

I would rebid 1NT over a 1 ♠ response but raise a 1 ♥ response to 2 ♥.

Jump raises always promise four trumps, but after being raised from one to two of his major, responder should never jump to four with only a four-card suit. One must get more information.

I suggest 2NT as an artificial inquiry (opener must not pass) over the single raise. In my scheme, the responses are easy to remember because they are generic. It doesn't matter what the minor or major is, the answers are the same. Another advantage is that responder's (declarer's) hand remains a mystery. If you can remember 3–3–4–4, you already know all the responses.

1 minor – Pass – 1 major – Pass; 2 major
   2NT = artificial inquiry with at least invitational values. Responses:
      3 ♣ = three-card support, minimum opener.
        3 ♦ = to play after a 1 ♦ opener.

3 ♦ = three-trump maximum, unspecified singleton, forcing to game. Next step (3 ♥) asks location of singleton. 3 ♠ = other minor; 3NT = other major.
3 ♥ = four trumps minimum no singletons, non-forcing.
  3 ♠ = to play (if spades was the suit).
3 ♠ = four-trump maximum, game-forcing, may have shortness. 3NT asks about singleton: 4 ♣ = none; 4 ♦ = other minor; 4 ♥ = other major.
3NT = three-trump maximum but no singletons.
4 of other minor = singleton in other minor, four-trump minimum.
4 of your minor = singleton in other major, four-trump minimum.
4 ♥ = 4–5–2–2 maximum.

2NT may be a game try or a slam try. Opener has 12–14 support points, having made only a single raise. So after the 2NT inquiry, 12-point hands will probably be minimums, 14s will be maximums and the 13s will require judgment. 2NT is at least a game-try, so all maximums are game-forcing.

Using 2NT as an inquiry rather than as a natural, non-forcing bid is useful for game and slam bidding. It allows you to determine the number of trumps, minimums versus maximums, while locating shortness. It allows you to feel a lot more comfortable raising partner with "only" three trumps. ❐

The author is a Diamond Life Master and two-time North American champion who lives and teaches bridge in Palm Beach Gardens FL.

I have also been fortunate to have been doing a monthly column in the Bulletin since January 2021, writing a series on various topics including Weak Two Bids in the 21st Century, The Many Faces of 4NT, Balancing, and others.

During the pandemic in 2020, I decided to try writing, and as of April 2022, have published 13 books on bridge, mostly on card play.

But I always wanted to write this book. Thanks to all my coaches and partners, some of whom unfortunately are no longer here.

It's been a great ride. I wouldn't have traded it for anything.

BRIDGE RESUME "DR. J"
JAMES MARSH STERNBERG, MD

THREE-TIME NATIONAL CHAMPION

1979   WINNER   MEN'S BOARD-A-MATCH TEAMS
1999   WINNER   BAZE SENIOR KNOCKOUT TEAMS
2012   WINNER   LEVENTRITT SILVER RIBBON PAIRS

1984   2ND PLACE   SPINGOLD KNOCKOUT TEAMS
2000   2ND PLACE   BAZE SENIOR KNOCKOUT TEAMS

WORLD CHAMPIONSHIPS

2014 SILVER MEDAL RAND CUP
   (WORLD CHAMPIONSHIP SENIOR TEAMS)

- Winner/Runner-Up of More Than 350 Regional & Sectional Tournaments
- 3-Time Florida Grand National Teams Champion
- 1985 United States Team: Icelandic Open
- 1990 Winner: Festivale Internazionale Di Bridge, Venezia, Italia
- Multiple High Finishes in World Championships in USA, Canada, France & Italy, including 4th place World Senior Championship: Montreal (2002) & Verona (2006)
- 2005/2006: USBF Coach USA Schools Team World Junior Championships
- 2009: USBF Coach USA Team World Youth Championships (2 WBF Bronze Medals)
- 2010: 2nd World Bridge Federation Senior Swiss Plate
- ACBL Diamond Life Master
- World Bridge Federation Senior International Master

Author: Many articles in bridge magazines; Bridge Bulletin monthly columnist since January 2021

- Author of 13 published bridge books
- Member: International Bridge Press Association
- ACBL Rookie of the Year 1977 (377 Masterpoints 1st Year); 20-year record
- Sponsor: Marsha May Sternberg Woman's Board-A-Match Teams Fall National Championships
- Bridge Biography in Encyclopedia of Bridge
- Trustee & Vice Chairman ACBL Charity Foundation: 2009–17, 2019–present
- Trustee ACBL Educational Foundation Committee: 2017–2018
- World Bridge Federation Medical Commission Member: 2018–Present

- Lifetime Member ACBL Charity Committee
- ACBL Certified Teacher (TAP)
- Experienced Cruise Ship Bridge Director

Email: mmay001 @ aol.com

Printed in the United States
by Baker & Taylor Publisher Services